CREATE^{SM} your own LUCK

Advanced Praise

"I've seen her speak, I've read her work, I've been in a hot tub with her. Hyatt is the real deal. What she teaches is grounded in her own experience -- practical actions and high-minded thought forms. Every chapter in Create Your Own Luck had me nodding, 'yep, yes, right on!' I adore how Susan approaches life. Take notes."

— Danielle LaPorte, creator of WhiteHotTruth.com and The Fire Starter Sessions

"During my own career as a self-help author, I've learned that we come in two varieties: the authors who write about the way they should be living, and the ones who write about the way they actually live. Many of the most glowing promises are made by the former group, but the truly useful strategies are delivered by the latter. I'm here to tell you that Susan is a walking embodiment of her own recommendations, a glowing, joyful, whip-smart, soft-hearted, hard-assed luckmeister."

— Martha Beck, Best Selling Author of Finding Your Own North Star and Steering By Starlight, www.marthabeck.com

"If you are serious about creating luck in your life, this mind-blowing book is about taking control of your life and your destiny - not leaving it to chance or circumstance. Susan explains that luck is not something that just happens nor is it sporadic but rather it's a way of setting up your life that invites luck in - permanently. if you want to be one of "those" people who you deem to be "lucky in life", this book will provide you with real-life examples and transformative step-by-step instructions on how to re-wire and electrify your brain to create oodles of long-lasting luck."

— Jackie Gartman, www.jackiegartman.com

Advanced Praise

"Susan Hyatt has a way of looking the impossible in the face and smiling it into submission. She helps you turn destructive thoughts into positive fuel, and will absolutely help your dreams come true. This book will change the trajectory of your life, guaranteed."
- Pamela Slim, author, Escape from Cubicle Nation: From Corporate Prisoner to Thriving Entrepreneur, www.pamslim.com

"Do not read this book. It's dangerous. You cannot get the ideas and exercises out of your mind - and heart. Which means you'll actually take action to change your life - no more excuses. No more saying "Tomorrow" or "When I lose the weight." You about to become very, very lucky. Don't say I didn't warn you."
- Jennifer Louden, best-selling author of The Woman's Comfort Book and The Life Organizer , www.jenniferlouden.com

"There's no one better than Susan Hyatt to help teach you how to get your lucky on. She showed me how to intentionally create the kind of day I want by Dialing It Up rather than ping-ponging through whatever life tosses at me. Susan is a force of nature and I always wondered how she creates all the "awesomesauce" in her life--this book is her awesomesauce recipe. Grab a copy like I did and start creating your life and luck using her practical, concrete, and most importantly, fun tools. And then put your lucky boots on and hold on for the ride."
- Bridgette Boudreau, Master Life Coach and CEO, Martha Beck Inc., www.weightshiftcoaching.com

A Little Lucky Note

Create Your Own Luck is about opening your mind and doing the work to bring more luck into your life. Because attorneys also like to get lucky, just understand that working through all of the Lucky Labs does not mean that you are going to win the lottery next week, find a bag of money lying in the street tomorrow, or be invited by Oprah to star on her new network, OWN. All kidding aside, this book was created as a reference tool. I am sharing my skills, knowledge and training with you with the intention that you will use the tools to bring more luck into your life. Along the way, I'd love for you to find your passion, have a clearer vision, work on your leadership, look for the WOW, dial up your creativity, and be 37 different kinds of awesome! If you can't, won't, or don't accomplish these things, I cannot be held responsible for this, nor can my publisher. Let's have some fun! Go whip up a smoothie and make yourself some MIND FUEL!

XO,

Susan Hyatt

CREATE your own LUCK ℠

SUSAN HYATT luck creator

7 steps to get your lucky on!

Journey Grrrl
PUBLISHING

Published by Journey Grrrl Publishing, Washington DC
Journey Grrrl Publishing, and the road meets the horizon design are regis-tered trademarks of Becoming Journey, LLC.

ISBN-13: 978-1-9369-8405-3
Library of Congress Control Number: 2011940934

Cover Design by Drai Bearwomyn
Cover Design Collaboration Lautaro Cabrera
Create Your Own Luck logo by Chelsea Sanders, Blueline
Interior Design by Karen Leigh Burton/Poodles Doodles

How to get your Free Gifts!

As a way of saying thanks for buying Create Your Own Luck, we are pleased to offer you $292.07 worth of FREE Gifts to accompany the book. Throughout the book, author Susan Hyatt offers Lucky Lab worksheets to help you create your own luck. Susan has also made available companion videos for each chapter and songwriter McCall Erickson wrote a special song just for you!

When you register at www.CreateYourOwnLuckBook.com, you'll receive all the following Lucky Items:

- » Lucky Song — Get Your Lucky On by Songwriter McCall Erickson
- » Lucky Lab#1 — Scientist in Your Life
- » Lucky Lab #2 — Track the Triggers
- » Lucky Lab #3 — Got Babemba?
- » Lucky Lab #4 — The Talent Ferret
- » Lucky Lab #5 — Envy Buster
- » Lucky Lab #6 — The Happy Basket
- » Lucky Lab #7 — Passion Formula
- » Lucky Lab #8 — Be Your Own Fun Coordinator
- » Lucky Lab #9 — Dial it Up
- » Lucky Lab #10 — Texts from God
- » Lucky Lab #11 — The Anti-Leotard Exercise Program
- » Lucky Lab #12 — What's Your End Game?
- » Lucky Lab #13 — Play to Your Edge
- » Lucky Lab #14 — Line Up Key Areas
- » Lucky Lab #15 — Line Up with Your Brilliance
- » Lucky Lab #16 — Inspiration Junction for Creativity
- » Lucky Lab #17 — What's Your Flavor of Fun?
- » Lucky Video 1 — How to Rock Your Day Using the Dial It Up Method!
- » Lucky Video 2 — Interview on Passion with Jessica Steward
- » Lucky Video 3 — Interview on Energy with Kimberly Kingsley
- » Lucky Video 4 — Luck, Leadership and Wealth, Interview with Kirsten Marion
- » Lucky Video 5 — Creativity and Luck Interview with Lisa Sonora Beam
- » Lucky Video 6 — Have more Fun and get Luckier, Interview with Ingrid Arna
- » Lucky Bonus — The Lucky 7 Manifesto

**Go to www.CreateYourOwnLuckBook.com
to download your free gifts today!**

-For Scott-

Who embodies the best kind of Luck

Table of Contents

Foreword

I've always known it was one of my lucky days when Susan Hyatt decided to sign up for my life coach training course. Another one came along when Susan decided to push her training to the level of Master Coach, and another when she agreed to work with me training other coaches.

Here's what I didn't know about all that luck: I did it! That's right—by writing this book, Susan has now convinced me that her very arrival in my life was luck I made my very own self (read on to find out how). At the time, of course, I didn't know how I was creating so much luck. I did it the same way I once made a rented Plymouth cruise gently down a hill in a sleepy neighborhood and park itself on a neighbor's lawn, with a combination of grim, sweaty effort and total bewilderment. But now, having read Create Your Own Luck, I can see the patterns. I can skip the grimness and replace bewilderment with understanding. And I believe I can begin replicating the luckiest things in my life with more precision and predictability.

During my own career as a self-help author, I've learned that we come in two varieties: the authors who write about the way they should be living, and the ones who write about the way they actually live. Many of the most glowing promises are made by the former group, but the truly useful strategies are delivered by the latter. I'm here to tell you that Susan is a walking embodiment of her own recommendations, a glowing, joyful, whip-smart, soft-hearted, hard-assed luckmeister. I've watched Susan encounter huge challenges in her personal and professional life, devising responses that always allowed her to ride the wildest waves of fortune like a ping-pong ball. I've watched luck come to her in ways others saw as random—and I've seen that actually, the strategies she teaches in this book were the driving force behind her success. My academic background always makes me demand real-world evidence for any self-help claim. Susan's life is her evidence.

Because she operates within a sort of coaching "tribe," Susan is also able to immediately test and refine her ideas with other savvy people. Their experiences, and those of clients who've used Susan's techniques under guidance from many different coaches, create an impressively sizeable pool of real evidence that Susan's "get your luck on" strategies yield results. Many, many people have already achieved impressive results using each tool she offers, and her clear, memorable instructions make it easy for her readers to benefit in the same way.

This is also just a fun read. When Susan says that to have fun you have to BE fun, she's speaking from a lifetime of experience. Just being near Susan is so much fun I'm sure there must be laws against it in many states. Her buoyant spirit shines through everything she does, and this book is no exception. So if you just now picked up Create Your Own Luck, prepare for a jolly, limit-smashing, thought-provoking, fascinating ride. Take it from me: having Susan Hyatt walk into your life, in person or in print, makes you one lucky reader. And about to get a whole lot luckier.

Martha Beck

Introduction

My nine-year-old daughter Emily loves to paint. She paints several times a week, sketches ideas, asks for gift certificates to the art shop over toys. It's her thing. Last year she entered a school-wide art contest. Students could enter any creative medium they wanted, including pottery, photography, video, paint, etc. The biggest criterion was that whatever they enter, it must incorporate the theme, "WOW."

Emily won a big blue first place ribbon, and her painting was entered into the state competition. One of her cousins came over and saw the giant ribbon on the refrigerator and commented, "Lucky!"

But was she lucky? Was it luck that she bought the canvases and materials? Was it luck that prompted her to ask that we take her to a local art studio so that she could consult with her favorite art teacher about how best to paint her idea? Was it luck that she spent hours sketching an idea and then painting it? Was it luck that created a zany painting idea of the Mona Lisa holding her cat Mango, surrounded by lightning bolts and fire flies? (WOW.) Let's back it up a bit.

Emily had a good attitude about entering the contest. She had a clear vision of what WOW meant to her and what she would paint. She sought out the supplies and help that she needed to get the work completed. So, when she won, it was nice recognition for something far greater than luck. It was a wonderful blend of clarity in belief, action, and the overall vision.

We are here on this planet to go deep within ourselves and experience our truest selves. If you agree to go within, you will experience joy on so many levels that people around you will wonder, "How did she get so lucky?!" And, with the tools and simple formulas in this book, you will be able to tell them and help them get lucky, too."

Lucky Quiz

Luck is not random. It's created.

My observations have led me to create a lucky litmus test when working with clients who want to create new results in their lives:

Are they clear? If not, are they open to getting clear?
Are they aware of what they are thinking?
Do they have passion?
Will they work?
Do they have energy?
Do they have vision?
Are they a leader? Can they lead?
Are they looking for a company/structure/government/person to give success to them, or are they willing to stand alone and paint outside the lines?

Take this simple and quick quiz to gauge your Luck Factor. Circle the word that best describes you.

I am genuinely excited about my future.

Always   Usually   Sometimes   Rarely   Never

When I get stuck, I seek out solutions (research, mentors/advisors) to help me.

Always   Usually   Sometimes   Rarely   Never

I usually get what I want.

Always   Usually   Sometimes   Rarely   Never

I consider myself resourceful. I can create new ways to solve a problem.

Always   Usually   Sometimes   Rarely   Never

I know exactly what to do to get what I want.

Always   Usually   Sometimes   Rarely   Never

People often look to me to make the decisions at home, work, or in social situations.

Always   Usually   Sometimes   Rarely   Never

I am grateful for my life.

Always   Usually   Sometimes   Rarely   Never

I tell the truth when people ask for my opinion.

Always   Usually   Sometimes   Rarely   Never

I put in the necessary time and energy to achieve what I want.

Always   Usually   Sometimes   Rarely   Never

Ideal Life Design
www.ideallifedesign.com

Lucky Quiz

I say no to things that I do not want to do.

    Always   Usually   Sometimes   Rarely   Never

I pay attention to what I am thinking and telling myself.

    Always   Usually   Sometimes   Rarely   Never

I feel energized in the middle of the day.

    Always   Usually   Sometimes   Rarely   Never

I am happy.

    Always   Usually   Sometimes   Rarely   Never

I have interests that I get involved in.

    Always   Usually   Sometimes   Rarely   Never

I have intimate relationships and feel connected to my loved ones.

    Always   Usually   Sometimes   Rarely   Never

I truly like who I am.

    Always   Usually   Sometimes   Rarely   Never

I value my opinion and what is important to me over others' expectations.

    Always   Usually   Sometimes   Rarely   Never

I spend time reflecting/mediating/praying in silence daily.

    Always   Usually   Sometimes   Rarely   Never

Award yourself 5 points for every ALWAYS • Award yourself 4 points for every USUALLY
Award yourself 3 points for every SOMETIMES • Award yourself 2 points for every RARELY
Award yourself 1 point for every NEVER

Total Score
_____

Scoring Key

So what's your gut telling you about your score? You probably don't even need to score yourself on luck. You already know. What's fun about a little quiz time is that it can help identify the potholes in your lucky landscape. Maybe you are a strong leader, but we need to amp up your creativity. Or, you are having lots of fun, but lack a clear vision for your future.

95—75	74—59	58—39	38—19
Clover-licious. Wow! Things seem to "always work out for you." I'm sure you hear that a lot. NOW, you will be clear about WHY, and how you can build on your luck to create even more abundance and joy.	It feels pretty good to be you most of the time. You are used to creating what you want. Let's crank up the volume so you play to your lucky edge even more.	You've got some good things happening, but only about half of the time. Let's find the lucky leaks in your life and amp up some more deliciousness.	Are you ready to ditch your current drama and create what you want? If you are interested in creating something different for yourself, buckle up and get ready. Your personal revolution begins now.

i Ideal Life Design
www.ideallifedesign.com

Chapter 1: Clarity

"I want to see how lucky, Lucky can be I want to ride with my Angel and live shockingly I want to drive to the edge and into the sea I want to see how lucky, Lucky can be."
Melissa Etheridge

So, what is luck then? If we ditch the notion that fortune is random and we embrace our own responsibility for creating it, luck is defined like this:

Luck is where the consistency of a good attitude, diligent work, and clear vision collide. It is clarity in belief, action, and the overall vision for your life.

Notice the word CLARITY in my definition. I've never met a truly lucky person who was not also clear about what they want. And, as you might guess, people who live from a space of clarity often admired as lucky. This is because they are not weighed down by thoughts, excuses, and distractions for very long. They keep their eye on the ball.

What does luck actually FEEL like? The moment that the luck trifecta blends, it feels like deep validation, a release of a tremendous knowing, and very, very delicious. But it does not feel like candy. It feels like a richly nourishing meal. A meal that was not served to you by another, but a recipe created and cooked by yourself. The process is a reward in and of itself, and the meal is a terrific result.

Personally, I have gotten so used to creating what I want in my life, that when I get it, it feels like, "Of course." But this wasn't always the case. I spent many years having success in one area or another, but never an authentic and peaceful existence in all areas of my life. I might have had a rockin' professional life some years, but my personal life was in jeopardy. Or, my spirituality was in question. And usually, my health was ignored.

I spent way too much time having adult temper tantrums, whining, using food as an escape, and looking outside of myself for my answers. I wasn't very good at playing the victim, but sisters and brothers I am here to say that I had the role of MARTYR down pat. It sucked. That crazy belief system included: "I have to do everything around here. No one works as hard as me. I sacrifice everything for my family. I can't relax because I have to be the one to keep it all together. " I was a rape survivor, my son was labeled with ADHD, I hated my job. Life wasn't "fair" to me.

The biggest lessons in my life have taught me – and new challenges continue to provide evidence – that luck and peace and harmony do not pull into the driveway and honk three times. I go out and catch them.

TURNING INWARD:

My mom was visiting for Easter when everything culminated for me. I was overworked and undernourished, and emotionally on edge. She offered to keep the kids for the day so that I could go out and have some fun by myself. I stopped and cried. I had no idea what I would do for fun. I had become so disconnected from myself that I wasn't sure what I would do with that time. In all honesty, grocery shopping and getting caught up on the laundry was about all I could think of.

It was in that moment that I decided. I knew deep down that there was a better way to live and love and contribute to the world. I had had enough experience with success in different areas of my life that I knew that I had it within me to discover a way to blend everything into a more satisfying and happy way of life. I decided to get to work on my inner life with the same gusto that I had applied to other successful areas of my life. And I was astounded by what I found.

I became a Scientist in my own life. I was fascinated with what worked and what didn't. I made a list of what felt good in my life. What was working? What didn't work? What could be better?

This is what my list looked like:

This is Working	This Needs to Be Better
Relationship with Scott	Time off to have fun
Relationship with kids	School for Ryan
Income	The way that I earn my income
	Weight (need to lose 25 lbs)
	Positive discipline with Ryan
	Spirituality

Looking back on this list, it is amazing to me how many things I have accomplished since then. I remember being a little afraid to take a look at things. But I knew that the alternative was more of them same. It became painfully clear to me that I needed to repurpose the skills I had used to build a business to rebuild my life. I wanted something more. And, if you are reading this book, it's a good bet that you want something more, too.

If you are afraid to turn inward and evaluate things, ask yourself why. Consider what your life will look like a year from now, five years from now, twenty-five years, and so on if you do not address these important life issues. They will fester. The pain will grow. That's what happens when we let pain drive the bus and we take a backseat. You are not a passenger in your life. Stop acting like one.

This first step is essential to the Luck Formula. You have to turn toward your life and really think about all areas before you can move forward to a luckier tomorrow.

Try this user-friendly exercise to be the Scientist in Your Life.

Scientist in Your Life

This is WORKING in MY Life: _____

_____

These areas could be BETTER: _____

_____

If I do not address these ISSUES:

What will these areas look and feel like one year from now? _____

_____

Five years from now? _____

Twenty five years from now? _____

Which area CONCERNS me the most? _____

_____

Frame Challenge Positively

(For example, instead of stating: "I hate my job!", say something more positive such as: "I will find work that I am passionate about that also creates excellent income.)

Why is this important to ME? _____

_____

How will I FEEL once I have created this? _____

_____

What can I think and do to DIAL UP this feeling state now? Ideas: _____

_____

_____

www.ideallifedesign.com

The next step is to look at your list of what could be better. Which one do you most want to address? Pick the one that you worry about the most. The one that keeps you awake at night. Look at each issue objectively, one by one, like a Scientist. By shining light on each issue, you can turn each one on its side and see solutions that were not clear before. How can you reframe your answers to create a list of the TOP 5 Things that YOU DO want?

EXAMPLE:

» *"I hate my job." Flip it around and it becomes: "I need to discover work that fills me up and also earns a good income."*

» And then ask yourself the priceless question: Why? Why is this important? How will it feel once you have this? What will it look like specifically?

» Use the worksheet to take each area that needs improvement, flip it to highlight what you do want, find out WHY, and discover how you will feel once it is a reality. Feel lucky? Good.

Getting clear is all about knowing what you truly want, and why you want it, and making sure that it is all in alignment with the lifestyle and values that you treasure.

People who are decidedly lucky have many things in common. But I believe that there is one exceptional quality that Luckies have in common. It's the most important quality because everything else flows from it. That quality is the ability to generate MIND FUEL.

MIND FUEL: Momentum produced by creating and believing good-feeling thoughts.

After you have turned toward your life, identified what you want, become clear about why you want it and how you want to feel, it will be very simple to create what you want. This is how: You learn to generate mind fuel. It is the single most important tool in this entire book. Pay attention here, because this is important.

Your beliefs fuel whether or not you take action and the kind of action that you take. Are you:

» too tired to plan?

» too busy to follow through on your plans?

» working very hard with little result?

If you answered yes, I guarantee that you are low on mind fuel. In fact, you are probably operating on mind crack.

MIND CRACK: *Quick fix action created by crappy thoughts that gives in to immediate pleasure but is dangerous to your long-term goals.*

A real life example: I had a weight loss client named Ellen. Ellen was truly committed to her mind crack stories about why it was so difficult for her to lose weight:

"All the women in my family are overweight so I am destined to be heavy no matter what I do."
"I don't have time to exercise and eat right."
"Nothing ever works for me."
"I never follow through on things."
"I'm a food addict and there is no help for people like me."

Ellen was so committed to these beliefs that she could not imagine any way out. You can see how when she believes thoughts like these, this will impact how she feels, acts, and her ultimate life result.

For Ellen, holding so tightly to these mind crack beliefs had some pay-offs for her. She could use these beliefs as excuses and never have to do any work on herself. They allowed her to hide behind the veil of weight and not show up in her life, which was scary for her. And, she was able to remain comfortable in her role of victim. Happy? No. Clear? No. Familiar? Yes.

Ellen's mind crack led to temporary pleasure, like visiting Whole Foods and eating a whole container of a dozen cupcakes, going out with friends and drinking bottles of wine, taking multiple trips to expensive spas to get away from it all, and blaming her husband and father for belittling her. All of these were pleasurable in the short term and damaging in the long term.

From Mind Crack to Mind Fuel

Step ONE Observe

So how do you change this? How do you transition from running on empty with Mind Crack to operating from a rich and nourishing place of Mind Fuel? The first step is to continue your role as Scientist in your life. This time, instead of observing in generalities what works and what doesn't, you'll be eavesdropping on yourself. There's a stadium full of opinions in your head, and it's shouting and gossiping and commenting and making snarky remarks all day and night long. It's time to tune into what you are telling yourself.

Things to remember when you begin this experiment:

You'll be flooded with thoughts. Most likely, you'll be shocked at the volume of things that you think. I always joke that I had immediately solved my exhaustion problem when I started observing my thoughts! I would never have said such things out loud to my worst enemy!

You are not your thoughts. Thoughts happen. It's the mind's job to think. But you are separate from them. Just because you have revenge fantasies about boxing your ex in the jaw does not make you a horrible person.

Be interested, curious, and fascinated. A Scientist always observes and never judges. When the flood comes in, be easy with yourself. Do not scold yourself. Just be fascinated with your mind.

It gets better. Really. With practice, it gets quieter and kinder in there.

Yes, it's normal. When left unattended, the mind is creative, elaborate, and destructive. Time to weed-eat.

What will you need?

Supplies for this are simple. Get yourself a nice journal/notebook/sketch book that will fit in your purse, backpack, briefcase, or will be easy to carry. It doesn't need to be expensive but it should feel important and special. Pick out something that you will like holding and using. Of course, you'll need something to write with. And, lastly but most importantly, an open mind. Be open to the possibility that these techniques will help you.

Easy ways to tune into what you are thinking:

I. **Take 15 in the morning.** Fifteen minutes in the morning is really all that you need to pop a clue about the crazed squirrel living in your head. Skeptical? Try it and you'll see what I mean. Before your day takes off, sit down in absolute quiet with a notebook. Write down every single thought that goes through your brilliant mind. It might not look so brilliant. In fact, if you are like me, it might look something like this:

And on, and on, and on. And on. But what you'll be doing is noticing themes, patterns, and sandwiched in there between the laundry and the peanut butter,

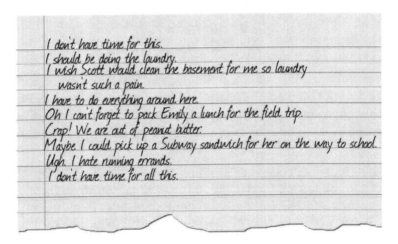

you'll find thoughts that are MIND CRACK, like "I have to do everything around here." I know, I know, you want to tell me that you DO do everything around here, and I will address your fantasies in a few pages. For now, we are just noticing.

2. **Stop every hour on the hour and listen.** Set your cell phone alarm, get a watch, or wind up an old fashioned egg timer. Just be committed to pausing once an hour and tuning in. The alarm goes off, and you put on your Scientist hat. Buzz. What am I thinking right now? Does it feel good? Interesting. Good to know. Write it down.

3. **Bad feelings are a cue to pay attention.** Anytime you experience a negative feeling STOP and pay attention to it. Don't drive through McDonald's, plow through Macy's, or belly up to the bar to avoid it. Notice this. It's important. What are you thinking that's creating the negative feeling? Make notes.

4. **Commute time reveals clues.** I love rockin' out to The Black Eyed Peas as much as anybody, but when you are trying to create a habit of observing your thoughts, keep the music and cell phone off when you are commuting. In the car, the subway, the trolley, the bus, your ten-speed. For now, until you get really good at noticing what you are thinking, when you are on the move, you are tuning into your mind instead of iTunes. What's it sound like? Put it in your notebook.

5. **Psycho Mode means it's time to tune in.** When you are DOING something that you know is not healthy, time to stop and observe. Me? Psycho? Never. What about last week when you grounded your kid for the rest of his life for not cleaning his room? Or, yesterday when your coworker asked you to cover for her and you said yes but secretly plotted to poison her coffee. Yes, that stuff. Notice it when you are in the middle of acting this way and track it back to the thoughts causing it. More for your growing pages.

From Mind Crack to Mind Fuel

Step TWO Evaluate Unlucky Thoughts

You've spent some time with your Scientist hat on observing and making notes. Now, it's time to evaluate your findings. Were you surprised? Me too. Isn't it just amazing what our unattended minds will cook up, spin, toss and scramble in there?

It's Good to Notice

» Repeat Offenders. These are thoughts that come up over and over again. You'll want to take special note of these "hot buttons." Things like:

» THAT Girl Syndrome. I had a client who was always comparing herself

> I don't have enough time.
> No one likes me.
> I do everything around here. (My personal favorite.)
> No one respects my time.
> Money is tight.
> Why can't I lose weight?
> They don't appreciate me.

to her friends and colleagues. She was never pretty enough, smart enough, thin enough, witty enough, and in her mind, she wanted to be THAT girl.

In my client's mind, THAT Girl was any member of her circle of model friends. So, while my client was out with her crew, she would spend the entire time telling herself that she didn't measure up. Her inner dialog started while she was getting ready. "Sure, I'm fashionable, but not as trendily delicious as everyone else that will be there. And, no guys will be even looking at me, so why bother? Everyone will be admiring and staring at my friends. I can't hold a candle to them. It's not fair."

So, my client would think herself into a sweaty mess, not make eye contact with new people, especially men, and this eventually would prove her thoughts true. No one was interested because she thought herself into a wallflower state. It's hard to ask someone out when they are busy hiding – metaphorically and quite literally.

THAT Girl Syndrome is the constant comparison of yourself to others. Funny thing is, there is only one you. Looking outward and comparing is the mind's way of seeking MIND CRACK evidence. It's not real. And, it's ridiculous. So notice it and be aware if this is a habit.

» How does she get all that done?

» Look at how thin she is.

» We are the same height. I should weigh what she weighs.

» My kids aren't as well dressed/fed/behaved as her kids.

» She has way more education/money/friends/boy toys than I do.

Victim Talk. This is MIND CRACK at its finest. Are you constantly whining in your head that you are treated so unfairly? That you have no idea what you ever did to deserve all this because you are a good person? That you can't make changes or do what you want because some relationship, job, town, or your childhood won't let you? Listen up! Because this is not only good to know, it is crucial. Not sure? See if you recognize yourself below.

○ I was abused as a child and that's why relationships will never work out for me.

○ I just can't figure anything out. I'm doomed.

○ My mom put me on a diet when I was five and told me that I was fat so that's why I am fat now.

○ I was raised Catholic/Jewish/Protestant/Wiccan and that's why I'm so confused.

○ My family didn't have the money to send me to college so I am stuck in this job that I hate.

Operating on victim-laced mind crack involves giving away your power and ability to someone else. There is no power outside of your own self that keeps you from what you want. Only mind crack that you leave unattended can do that.

"The past is a foreign country. They do things differently there."
LP Hartley

» Martyrdom. This was my MIND CRACK of choice. The sacrificial victim. You think the world would stop spinning without you because you do "everything for everybody." You shove your own needs to the back burner to save everyone else, and then bitch that you don't get to do what you want to do.

- o I drive these kids around from activity to activity and have no time to work out.

- o I'm so tired of being the only one to pick up/pay bills/fold laundry around here.

- o Last week I worked an extra 10 hours on that project and no one said thank you.

- o It would be nice to take a vacation but I can't because mother needs me.

- o These pets/tomato plants/composting worms/humans would literally STARVE TO DEATH if I were not here to make sure they were fed.

» How much time do you spend lamenting, complaining, and plotting your escape? Imagine spending that time operating on MIND FUEL and getting what you want. It's more fun.

» How does it feel? Simply put, do these thoughts feel good or bad? Do they make you want to run a marathon or run and hide? Isn't it fascinating to notice how often we give away our power to something outside of ourselves? In the words of the little Taco Bell dogs, "No Mas! Viva Chihuahuas!" Ok, little joke. But seriously. No more. It's time to live.

Track the Triggers

Track the triggers. Noticing the people, places and things that trigger negative thoughts can be helpful. These will be considered potential challenges in the future, and by aknowledging them, you can prepare and have some good feeling thoughts ready in advance. We'll dive into that more in Step 3. For now, just track them.

Based on one week of keeping your journal...

What was happening that triggered this kind of thinking? (Example: My boss gave me an unreasonable deadline.) _____

_____

Where were you? (at work) _____

Who were you with? (Alone after meeting with boss) _____

What thoughts were you thinking? Can you remember what you told yourself that triggered that behavior? (This isn't fair, I'll never get it done on time. I hate this job.) _____

_____

What emotions were you feeling or avoiding? (Angry, hopeless, irritated) _

Did you feel it in your body? If yes, where? (stomach, shoulders, headache) _____

What was the end result? (I ate a whole bag of Doritos and later felt sick)_

Did you notice certain people, places, or situations that trigger negative thinking? _____

"Do you believe you're a victim of a big compromise? Cause I believe you could change your mind and change our lives."
John Mellencamp

From Mind Crack to Mind Fuel
Step THREE Cooking with Mind Fuel

Creating thoughts that line up with what you want involves some creativity. But, you'll feel so good once you get the hang of this practice, you'll want to keep it up. Let's take a look at your repeat offenders and the thoughts that you've observed that are the most worthy of the MIND CRACK award. Pick 5 of them and plug them into the worksheet below. Then, in the right hand column, plug in the things that you said that you really, really, really wanted.

Top 5 Mind Crack Thoughts	Top 5 Things I Want
1. _____	1. _____
2. _____	2. _____
3. _____	3. _____
4. _____	4. _____
5. _____	5. _____

Notice anything? Can you see how if you entertain the MIND CRACK on the left, you will never get what you want on the right? They are in direct opposition to one another.

Let's look at just one. I'll use one from my journal.

Mind Crack Thought	Desired Result
I don't have enough time to get this all done	Have a productive day

If I entertain the thought, "I don't have enough time," and leave it unattended, it will create a sensation of panic and anxiety in my chest. I will look at my planner over and over and lament over everything that I have to do. I become cranky. I snap at my loved ones during breakfast. I decide not to exercise because there is "no time." Ultimately, my day is far from productive. What I do get done only receives a fraction of the energy and passion inside of me. I've given all of it to the mind crack.

But if I take that thought, and shine my light all over it, I can come up with some MIND FUEL that will serve me better. It takes some creativity to massage an icky thought into one that inspires you to do and feel better. Play with it. Let's try together.

Tips for Mind Fuel Creation:

Don't try to make big jumps. The biggest mistake that I see with clients learning how to create mind fuel, is that they try to jump from depressed to elated in one big thought jump. You usually won't believe it's possible, and it will feel like a waste of time. For example, if I am currently thinking, "This job sucks," trying to convince myself that "I really love this job," is not going to work, no matter how brightly I fake a smile when I say it. Play around and find thoughts that are just a bit better than the previous thought and build from there.

Check out the Mind Crack to Mind Fuel evolution below:

This job sucks.» I work because I value paying my bills.» This job doesn't have to be permanent.» I can find work that fulfills me.

Notice that I did not try to say that "This job doesn't suck" or "Ain't I lucky to have this crappy job?" I turned my attention toward what I wanted, and broke it down into little shifts in thinking.

Be patient. Rome wasn't built in a day. And these mind crack belief systems were not developed overnight, either. Be patient with yourself as you learn to notice what you are thinking and begin to design Mind Fuel. It takes some practice, but you are totally up for it.

Get creative. At first, this will feel awkward. But it helps to get creative with your thinking by concentrating on what you want. There are many ways to get that thing that you want. And there are many thoughts you can think. Try these little techniques below, using the example thought, "I don't have enough time to get this done."

» Throw it out.
  I don't have to get all this done today.

» Turn it on its side.
  There's always enough time for me.

» Get laser focused.
  Just this. I only have to do just this in front of me.

» Flip it around.
  Of course there is enough time.

Now take the new thoughts that you created and sit with them. Do they make you feel better? If not, go back and keep trying until you find one that created a good feeling shift in you. You'll know it when you feel it.

One last tip here. It is quite common to find a creative replacement thought, feel relief, and have the same damned thought resurface the next day, the

34

next hour, the next minute. The thought may resurface exactly the same, or as a "cover thought" along the same theme. Your replacement thought may not give you the same relief that it did before. You are not doing anything wrong.

I'd like to report that once you replace a thought with something that feels good, that it will stick and you will be cured of this negative mind crack forever. Unfortunately, this isn't how the brain works. (There are many experts who can explain to you exactly how the brain functions in a thorough and scientific way. I am not one of those people. If you want the step-by-step scoop, a great book to read is My Stroke of Insight by brain scientist Jill Bolte Taylor, PhD.)

Here's my simple explanation. When you have years of thinking MIND CRACK thoughts, like, "I never finish anything," you have a huge list of evidence that you've collected in your crack pipe. Every time you didn't finish a book, a soap opera, a French fry, your fast-moving mind made note of that to support the belief. This is simply what the mind does. Now that you are choosing to create MIND FUEL beliefs, your list of helpful evidence is naturally slim. You just haven't been working on it as long as the crummy belief. It's kind of like your mind has paved a smooth road called MIND CRACK EXPRESSWAY. And, at first, MIND FUEL AVENUE is like a brand new back road that is just being cleared for paving.

So, you have new directions. They feel good and solid. You turn onto the new road and hit a pothole. Your mind decides to turn back on MIND CRACK EXPRESSWAY because it's easy, it's familiar, and that's what it's always done. That's all. You aren't defective. You CAN do it. It just takes some intentional practice.

When you need some help generating MIND FUEL over MIND CRACK, think about the Babemba Principle. The Babemba are an African tribe with a wonderful tradition. When a member of this tribe does something that is considered offensive or wrong, the tribe members actually take the time to stop all activity and surround the person to take turns recounting all of the things that they remember where the person got it "right."

Babemba Principle
Got Babemba?

When you need some help generating MIND FUEL over MIND CRACK, think about the Babemba Principle. When a member of this African tribe does something that is considered offensive or wrong, the tribe members actually take the time to stop all activity and surround the person to take turns recounting all of the things that they remember where the person got it "right". Can you imagine working in corporate America, screwing up on a major account, and the company stopping all work to surround you and give you a pep talk? Me either. The great news is that you don't have to wait around for other people to give you props. Give it to yourself. When you notice the signs of MIND CRACK, it's time to implement your own Babemba Principle.

The situation: Write a two sentence description of a negative situation that has happened. (What happened? Who was involved? What were the consequences?) _____

_____

Thinking about the situation: What are your MIND CRACK thoughts about this situation?_____

Does this feel good or bad? How does it feel specifically? _____

If you continue thinking these thoughts and feeling this way, how will your day be? _____

What can you learn from this situation?_____

How is the situation perfect for you? _____

Dial up some Babemba

Now instead of wallowing in the past, something that you cannot change, let's dial up some good feeling evidence that will better serve you in the right now. List 5 things.

you've done well in the last week	you've done well in the last month	you've done well in the last year	that are awesome about you
»	»	»	»
»	»	»	»
»	»	»	»
»	»	»	»
»	»	»	»

When you can successfully line up what you want, what you think, and what you do, you will be stunned by your luck.

A real life story.

I was recently bumped up to First Class on a return flight home to Indiana from Phoenix. (Lucky.) I was seated next to a woman who talked to me from the moment we were seated until we exchanged hugs and ran to catch our connecting flights.

I had planned on working on this book the entire flight. I had set the intention that I would spend the entire flight time making notes and writing. When Becky started talking, I had to shift gears. I was tired. I really didn't want to talk. But I noticed that I changed my thoughts and was thinking, "Writers are interested in people and life." And, I was. We started talking about where we had been and where we were going. Becky was flying from Phoenix where she was helping her daughter plan a wedding, back home to the St. Croix, an island in the US Virgin Islands. "How lucky," I thought. And, then, these few pages wrote themselves.

Becky had lived and raised a family in the great Midwestern city, Cincinnati, Ohio. When her children were little, she managed to build her own home, create a thriving event planning company that was the top company of its kind in town, and live a very lucky life. She and her husband would vacation on St. Croix many times before deciding that the island felt like home. Gradually, over a three-year period, they sold their properties, the business, and relocated to their island paradise.

In the three years that it took to pick up their roots, real estate values skyrocketed. Did they lament, cry, and whine? Nope. They started talking to locals. And, luckily, they become friends with someone who introduced them to someone who was literally island royalty, and offered them an oceanfront "guest house" (i.e. mansion) for rent. So here she was, living her island paradise dream on a 4.5 million dollar property with ocean front views, almost rent free. She found a great position planning events for a local resort, and life was good.

Eight months later, after noticing a small bloodstain in her bra, Becky discovered that she had breast cancer in both breasts. To receive adequate medical care, Becky found herself living back in the United States for 8-9 months. She lost both of her breasts. But, she successfully kicked cancer's ass and was able to return to St. Croix.

Here is what was fascinating to me. To listen to Becky tell this story, she told it, quite frankly, like a lucky person. She spoke of how LUCKY she was to detect the cancer herself. How fortunate she was be able to afford proper medical care. And, that even though she had to have her breasts removed, she was able to avoid chemotherapy and harmful drugs. Most importantly, she was grateful for the experience, because when she returned to the island, she realized that her great job wasn't what she really wanted to be doing with her life. She's had a brush with mortality, and it woke up something more in her. Becky was grateful that her friend cancer showed her how she wanted to live: in paradise, doing something more.

Becky thought it was funny how excited I became just listening to her talk. She had no idea that her example was evidence of lucky thinking at work. I explained to her that I have worked with many clients who would retell the story very differently. It might sound something like this:

> It took me three long years to sell off everything and finally get to St. Croix. And then, once I was able to move there and buy property, real estate prices were CRAZY high and we couldn't even afford anything. So, then, I was reduced to living in a rental. And to top it all off, I got cancer. It was so bad that it was in BOTH breasts, and I had to lose them. Can you imagine the pain of having to lose your womanhood like that? It nearly crushed me. After sacrificing and selling everything to move to my island paradise, there wasn't a single doctor there who could help me there. I had to go back the stinkin' main land for treatment. It took eight months of my life. It totally sucked. It was so horrible that when I got back to St. Croix, that I didn't even have the energy and interest to do my job. So, I ended up losing that gig and here I am without direction. Why do bad things happen to good people?

But for Becky, cancer in her journey was a gift. It was lucky and amazing. The only difference between her and "unlucky" people, are her thoughts about it. And, that is precisely why she lives happily, enjoying a lucky and charmed life, of her own design.

Chapter 2: PASSION

"In your memory there is a snapshot of a girl on an unstoppable mission to invent, create, take risks, and have fun!"
Kathy Vick *(Run Like a Girl)*

"There is no dishonor in losing the race. There is only dishonor in not racing because you are afraid to lose."
Garth Stein

Passion is essential to create your life and luck. It's is a direct byproduct of MIND FUEL. The flavor of this physical feeling state is sort of like the cumin in guacamole dip. It's a spicey, little something extra, exciting rumble in the gut. Passion radiates out from my core and I can feel my blood coursing through my veins to the end of my fingertips making little exclamation marks! This feeling state is created from consistent passionate thoughts that honor your core's deepest longings.

Passion does not simply materialize. It doesn't pull into your driveway and honk twice. It's not delivered by the stork or unwrapped during the holidays. It's the continuous turning toward things that pique your interest. It's that fire in the belly to do things regardless of the perceived obstacles, whether or not you are paid, and in spite of what our minds and others say is possible. You might have an affinity for something, but it will fizzle out and not bloom into passion if you aren't cooking with MIND FUEL.

And while passion is something to be nurtured, if you are being the Scientist of your life, and paying attention to what tugs at you, you might be truly and deliciously surprised at what you discover you become passionate about.

Last year, I had the pleasure of working with a group of entrepreneurs for an entire year to help them create their luck in business. I just love the passionate energy of business creation. It's better than chips and salsa to me. One of the participants, Jessica, was exceptionally gifted, but she was entertaining some super sized **MIND CRACK**.

I don't know if I can do this.
Who will hire me?
Can I make any money at this?

You get the drift. And obviously, leaving these kinds of thoughts alone to breed and multiply like those little psychotic gremlins is a recipe for having fancy business cards and no business.

Jessica had quite a bit of resistance to one of the homework assignments required for the program: create a video blog. Now, this in particular was pushing many of the program's participants to their edge. Not just the technology involved, but stepping up and being willing to learn how to be on camera, and put their talents out there in the world. Such a great homework assignment that triggered many issues for the class to work on: thoughts about worthiness, thoughts about body image and beauty, thoughts about being good enough.

But, what Jessica noticed as she investigated her resistance and did her work on shifting her MIND CRACK to MIND FUEL, was that her creativity exploded. (More on Creativity in Chapter 5.) She was able to tap into her gift, pulling together images, music, and content to tell a story. It was so much more than just "making a little video." This was art. And she had found her passion in an unexpected place.

Now? Jessica runs a wildly popular and successful Video Star series to help other small business owners own their video mojo.

"I was incredibly resistant to the whole idea at first. I believed that videos for coaches and small business owners with no budgets for video had to be a "talking head", blathering on at the camera for 3 minutes or more. I didn't know what to talk about and frankly, didn't believe I had anything new to say that would captivate my audience. I actually had resolved not to do it and risk my mentor's wrath.

There was a distinct part of me (I'll say my essential self) that said "break the rules, do something different." Giving myself permission to be different helped free me from the belief that I had to be a "talking head" and the ideas started percolating. I remembered these incredible Victorian party masks that were leftover from my wedding favors. I created stickers to put on the back of a James Baldwin quote:

"Love takes off masks that we fear we cannot live without and know we cannot live within."

When I thought of that, I realized that not only did I have an incredible prop, but also an incredible concept to convey. The idea of spinning in my chair with all the masks came to me, spinning reminded me of "roulette", roulette reminded me of Chat Roulette, that internet fad and how people could pretend to be something they aren't (or are?) and allowed them to unmask their inner freak.

I don't know how to explain it, but letting myself be different by revealing my long-slumbering creativity felt like stepping back into my power in many ways. I could feel the sizzle that the powerful message of my video conveyed. While I did have fear that people would hate it, there was a deep knowing that they'd love it because I loved it. And it worked. Once people saw that I was not only talented, but truly passionate about it, they wanted more from me. They wanted to learn from me. (me??) I decided to create a teleclass on helping others unleash their creative side in video, help them get over that hurdle of fear, and recognize the true power of creating not only an authentic message but one that shows the world how unique they really are. It's coaching in disguise. I felt so lucky that I happened to try out video and find people liked it.

But here's the deal...

I created this luck. I signed up for Susan's Clear Coaches class. I decided to embrace my differences and allow my creativity. I got over the limiting belief that since I'm not a professional video editor or producer I wouldn't have something important to contribute to others who want to embrace this medium. Real "luck" isn't happenstance. It's showing up, being willing to take a risk, and believing that you deserve the end results. What felt like something random and unbelievable was neither; I took the risk and I reaped the reward. That is truly lucky."

Jessica Steward www.stewardcoaching.com

So, get that vision of spending your "happily ever after" lounging on a beach sipping cosmos out of your head. You'll enjoy that for about a week and then be looking for something else to do. I'm convinced this is why many retirees are depressed. They haven't been taught about MIND FUEL and playing to their edge. They spent their lives being busy operating under the structure of a company and a boss, and without that structure outside of themselves, they are lost.

But far too many people are lost way before retirement. Corporate America is so jammed full of disillusioned MBAs that my friend Pam Slim wrote an entire book about it called *Escape From Cubicle Nation*. So, escape with me. What are you passionate about? Here's a clue. Your passion typically will reside in one of these categories:

* **Eureka!** It's the answer to some problem that once kept you awake at night. If you've ever met a reformed smoker, then you know what I'm talking about. In my experience, we are usually on fire to spread the word about something that solves a problem that we or our loved ones have faced. You found a way to get your colicky newborn to sleep? I bet you burn up the online forums to help parents and call all your friends to tell them.

* **Easy Peasy.** What are you ridiculously good at? What is such easy fun that you might miss thinking of it as a passion? It could be anything, it might be unusual, or it may appear like something that isn't that big of a deal. It doesn't have to be something obvious like painting, singing, math, sales, or belly dancing. It can be subtle.

When I was younger and nurturing a giant chip on my shoulder, I would watch Oprah for inspiration. (Some things never change. Oprah rocks.) But, when I would hear her say, "Find your passion and the money will follow," I wanted to jump off the nearest bridge. I did totally believe that money was the natural by-product of passion, and still do, but I also believed that I had no such talent and passion. I would watch the guests on her show who had made a gazillion dollars following their passion of writing, or baking cookies, or making purses out of old tires, and I'd wonder when my passion would find me. I thought that all I was really good at was reading and discussing books. For years I overlooked this as a talent. Turns out that I figured out how to turn that into a life coaching business. Go figure. Couple that with being really good at seeing other people's strengths and here I am. Passionate.

The Talent Ferret

A few years ago, my son Ryan begged me for a ferret for his 11th birthday. I was adamantly against it. Totally. Completely. It was not going to happen. We already owned two high maintenance beagles, one hairball prone cat named Mango, and two robo hamsters (whose cage was so disgusting that I am sure it is the origination of the swine flu).

Keep in mind that my children's birthdays are five days apart, so anytime there was a ferret debate, my daughter Emily would chime in with her request for a Parrot. For months the words ferret and parrot would bounce against the back of my head when we would be in the car together. It was a rhyming nightmare.

Ryan would state all the wonderful qualities of the ferret: they're cool, they're soft, they could be trained as spies for the CIA. I would say that I would rather buy him more violent and coma inducing XBOX 360 games, and he would say that he was certain we would get a ferret instead.

As it turns out, I underestimated Ryan's ability to manifest the impossible, and my husband's secret childhood desire to own a ferret. On Ryan's birthday, at approximately 4:45 p.m., on my husband's way home from work, he just happened to know where he could pick up an exotic ferret to bring home for the birthday dinner. And five days later, Emily became the proud owner of one, too. (The Parrot desire died in the face of a musky scented weasel.)

I tell you my tale of obnoxious animal ownership to demonstrate a few things. First, never doubt that passionate desire trumps "reality." Second, there is much to be learned from ferrets. Just when I thought I didn't want one, and was a little afraid of them, I discovered they are pretty awesome little pets. Ryan was right. They are not only very cool and soft, they are also resourceful, mischievous, persistent, and very, very playful.

Ferrets LOVE to play hide and seek, and they especially love to swipe SHINY objects and hide them. So, seeking is a big part of the ferret's life. They are more persistent than a dog with a bone, and will not give up until they've satisfied their undying curiosity. All of these qualities are critical to develop passion.

I invite you to ferret out your passion. It's wonderful and shiny and hidden right now. But you can dig it up very easily if you shape-shift into a ferret.

The Talent Ferret

What are you *ridiculously good at*? This could be anything: filing your finger nails, running, grocery shopping, creating playlists, or drinking coffee. Brainstorm here:

_____

_____

_____

What do you do *better then ANYBODY else*? Do you figure out the ending movies and books in the first few chapters? Do your friends take your with them when they buy a car because you are an expert negotiator? Are you the one in the neighborhood who always grows the tastiest tomatoes? Pay attention and make notes here:

_____

_____

_____

What triggers your *Little Green Monster*? I've learned that envy is really the evil twin of admiration. When you catch yourself feeling envious of someone, really pay attention to that feeling. It's typically about something that you crave in your own life, but your negative thinking gets involved and creates a belief that you want it but you cannot have it. Or, that since they have it, you cannot. Scarcity and Lies! Turn it to admiration. When have you felt intense jealousy lately? Write it down here:

_____

_____

_____

Go back through your answers and list the things that stand out to you here:

_____   _____

_____   _____

_____   _____

_____   _____

It's my belief that if we are capable of craving something in our lives, we are capable of creating some version of it within ourselves and in our lives.

I might admire NFL Quarterback Peyton Manning's athletic ability. Standing 5'3" and 120 pounds, it's a fact that I do not have the ability to be drafted into the NFL. Never. Gonna. Happen. But, looking deeper at what I really admire: his dedication, his hard work, his ability to leave it all on the field. He's smart, strategic, and agile. Now I'm getting someplace. I am also those things. I can create more of that, instead of lamenting that I can "never realize my dream of becoming an NFL Quarterback" and other silliness that we "drama up" in our minds.

Envy Buster

Envy is just admiration that has been *hijacked by MIND CRACK*. You spot it, cause you got it. Or, because you are capable to creating it. And envy is a great source of clues. Investigate your little green monster and see what I mean.
Name five people that you have found yourself jealous of *and why:*

1. _____

2. _____

3. _____

4. _____

5. _____

What do you *admire* about them (qualities, skills, etc.)?

_____

_____

What do you *think you crave* in your own life based on this?

_____

_____

How would you *feel* if you had what you admire in their lives?

_____

_____

How can you *create that for yourself*? What ideas do you have?

_____

_____

_____

_____

_____

Real life story. Eric is a guy who I am convinced must have a genius IQ. He came to me on the recommendation of his girlfriend who felt he needed a career tune up. And, let me just say that he was not at all digging the whole self-help arena. I think he used the adjectives "lame" and "cheesy" more than once. But, as soon as Eric discovered that I wasn't a crystal selling, unicorn riding, snake-oiled guru, he humored me.

The biggest issue and area of least satisfaction for Eric was that, in his words, he did not feel excited about life and was not passionate about anything. He had created a successful company in college that was bought out by European investors, and stayed on as a consultant for the past 20 years. He made excellent (read INSANE amounts of) money but was "bored." With the exception of his school-aged daughter, he felt lifeless.

After teaching Eric about MIND FUEL, we started working on Eric becoming a Scientist in his life, just like you did in Chapter 1. I remember him as partly cynical when I suggested that he could create passion, and that there were many things in this life that were entry points to create and fuel his passion. I pulled out the big guns for my sarcastic, genius of an engineer: the happy basket. He wanted to fire me.

The Happy Basket

The Happy Basket is a very simple tool that I use in my daily life and with clients. Don't let its simplicity fool you. It might be tempting to skip this step ... *don't*. I have had clients create entire businesses based on their Happy Basket results. At the very least, you will notice what works, what makes you smile, and that is something to make some time to savor. It's easy and takes very little time.

What did *you* find? List your Happy Basket results here:

What you need:

A medium or large basket (a laundry basket a wicker basket, or a big bowl are all fine)

Post-it notes

Pen

A set of observant eyes

An open mind

How to Happy Basket

- Put a basket in a high traffic location of your home and/or office. I keep mine in my kitchen.

- Everytime that something makes you happy and smile, it goes in the basket.

- Things that are too big to fit in the basket are written down on little post-it notes and the notes are placed in basket. (My basket typically includes things like magazine articles, photos, quotes, books, ticket stubs stories about my kids, and the funny things that they say, etc.

- "Do the Happy Basket" for a week or two

- Review the results and notice trends. For example, my basket's "happiness trends" are quiet time, kids, family, writing, coaching, hiking and learning.

So Eric was a good sport and did his Happy Basket assignment. And while he thought there wasn't much in his basket, we did notice a trend in the results. Eric was restoring an old townhouse in the DC metro area, and doing his best to make it as "green" as possible. As we talked, he realized that most things in his basket were about green living. And, he was pretty jacked up about this topic. Could it be passion brewing? You bet it was.

Once we opened that door, it was like race day at Saratoga. Within weeks, Eric emailed me a business plan for a company that manufactured wind blades for alternate energy windmills. It was totally over my head, but the graphics were cool so I knew he must be onto something. Within a few months, he had secured a private investor and two power companies to back his efforts. Today, his clients include the largest wind turbine blade supplier in the world. Yep, that's what a little passion will get you.

It's a great inspirational story, but I can hear you coming up with the reasons why Eric was just "lucky" and how this could never happen for you. In fact, I use Eric's story with almost every single client who hires me to discover passion and motivation in a career. This is what I hear from them in the beginning:

"Yea, but you said he was a genius. I'm not a genius."
"He lives in DC. I live in a small town. I could never make that happen."
"Well, I'm REALLY not interested in anything. I don't have any hidden passions like him."
"I have four kids and am a single mom. I don't have the time he has."

Let me stand on my soapbox now and yell into my megaphone, "THIS IS WHY LUCKY THINGS AREN'T HAPPENING FOR YOU!" Excuses are nothing more than fear dressed up. They look and seem reasonable so that you buy them, but they are in fact lies that keep you stuck. Knock it off already. Use Eric's story as an example of what IS possible instead of what isn't.

Passion Formula

Back to being a Scientist.
Notice the things in your life that are:

Simple Pleasures

Cravings Alert

Cultivate your cravings and interests:

_____

_____

_____

_____

Expand on the simple. Take it up a notch:

Design passion into your life. Challenge yourself — Stretch

Exhale. Have some fun:

_____

_____

_____

_____

www.ideallifedesign.com

How do I know that you aren't having enough fun? 'Cause I do. My clients and readers are incredibly smart and successful and witty and good looking. Right? But you probably have to schedule fun into your schedule or it doesn't happen. I can feel you nodding your head.

Have some fun. BE some fun. It's your true nature. Just like everything else, if you aren't having any fun, fun isn't going to smack you on the ass. You have to create fun. You have to BE fun. You are going to be your own fun coordinator. Let's take a look again at your Happy Basket results. List the top 5 things. How can you take things mentioned there and make an activity of them? Or, if it already is an activity, schedule consistent time doing it. How can you make it even better and MORE fun?

Be Your Own

Fun Coordinator

You aren't having enough fun and that's a crying shame. If life is just a series of check-marks in your planner, it's time to do something about it. What I've learned for sure that that *Fun is 100% necessary for luck*. In my opinion, it's as important as sleep.

Remember playing for hours, and your mom having to make you come inside to eat dinner? What did you love to do as a kid? Legos, dolls, rubix cube? Name 3-5 things here:

1. _____

2. _____

3. _____

4. _____

5. _____

Pick one thing ... why was that fun for you? What was cool about it?

_____

_____

Can you still do that, or create a grown-up version? List ideas here:

_____

_____

What's fun for you to do with a partner?
A group?
Solo?
Name three things that you have been interested in trying or doing, but you said you didn't have the time or the money.

1. _____

2. _____

3. _____

Pick ONE THING to try this week: this month:

Happy Basket Results	Fun Activity	Date Scheduled	Ideas to AMP it up
1.			
2.			
3.			
4.			
5.			

Now that we've got clarity and passion simmering, let's get to work on your energy in chapter three.

Chapter 3: Energy

***When your personality comes to serve the energy of your soul,
that is authentic power.***
Gary Zukav

Low energy equals bad luck. You can count on it. Your life energy is the most precious commodity you have. All of that annoying advice to get more sleep, and drink more water, and eat your Wheaties, and exercise (and to friend Susan Hyatt on Facebook) is actually really sound advice. But, I bet you didn't know that all of these little things add up to whether or not you are lucky.

Have you ever looked around in traffic, at the grocery store, or God forbid on the subway, and noticed the expressions of the people around you? It's a little scary. Their shoulders are hunched over; their eyes hold blank, sad expressions. What about you? I used to smile in meetings and cry at stop lights. I'd power through my work, but sleep through my real life. My energy reserve was running on empty.

If you walk around zoned out, tired, cranky, yawning instead of engaging in a meeting, closed off from ideas and feedback, just powering through the day, you can consider yourself blocked from the brilliance that is a given in your natural state. It's there, just buried. It's buried under mind crack, processed foods and lack of sleep. And it's a big nasty disconnect.

I totally get that right now, perhaps the only things that get you energized and excited are ice cream trucks or revenge fantasies about your mother-in-law. But stay with me here. Use all of that work that you did in Chapter Two and your Happy Basket Results to remember what excites you and gives you energy.

When I was a brand new realtor and building my real estate practice, I remember interviewing various business coaches. One coach in particular impressed me with his energy. I was struggling with managing a growing roster of clients and my family life. And yet, somehow he was able to own his own real estate office, manage over 200 agents, sit on the board of several not-for-profit organizations, and be active in his family's life. He worked fewer than 40 hours per week and earned a seven-figure income. As a young entrepreneur, I was amazed at his ability to achieve so much and maintain balance. I wrote him off as an anomaly. I told myself he was just "lucky."

I didn't get it then, but I totally get it now. He wasn't born with some "star quality" DNA that the rest of us do not have. He hadn't been given his success by inheritance. He had developed a lucky mindset that fueled unbelievable clarity and good-feeling energy. I could literally feel it when we talked on the phone.

So how do you generate positive energy? You can create it yourself, or rather, return to it—your natural state-- with some simple techniques that have taken me from unpredictable chaos to intentional connection.

First, there are a couple things you should know about me. I drink too much coffee (Seattle's Best #3, please) and I practically freebase green smoothies. Yes, I have a lot of energy. But believe it or not, my guilty pleasures are not the reasons I am so "jacked up" about things all the time. And by jacked up, I mean pumped up and feeling amazing.

I do not always wake up happy and excited, and I promise that I don't burp rainbows. I'm a regular mom who sometimes finds herself unsuccessfully chasing her beagle in the rain, scraping Emily's artistic creations off of the kitchen table, and trying to explain to her 12-year-old son that the movie American Pie (OMG) may not be live streamed from Netflix to his personal computer. This is why we lovingly refer to our home as the Hyatt Riot.

When I wake up to a beagle covered in green paint, or kids plotting to boycott school, I've learned that I can still create the feeling state that I want, if I'm open, willing and intentional. I can decide how my day will go, in spite of less than ideal (ok, crappy) circumstances. If I wake up anxious, or cranky, I can blend up a feeling state like I cook up a green smoothie. I mix in a little bit of excited, and a heaping helping of passion, and a dash of motivation.

How? I developed a strategy and routine to nourish and connect with my energy source.

It starts with a morning ritual that takes 15 minutes. You can take 15 minutes, right? Of course you can. It truly is the most important segment of your day.

Part of my morning ritual is my Dial It Up! Method. It's a fast and direct way to set my intention for the day. It helps me create good thoughts to generate the feeling state that helps me get what I want. Then, I line up some inspired action and knock off at least one thing that isn't serving me.

Dial It Up

Name it!

I'm not feeling so hot. In fact, I'm feeling pretty crappy.

What am I feeling exactly right now?

- _____
- _____
- _____

Decide it!

If I could pick any feeling to have about today, what would it be?

Better yet, I want to have a blend of these three cool feeling states.

- _____
- _____
- _____

Bring it!

What can I believe to DIAL UP these feelings for myself?

Ideas: _____

_____

What can do to help fuel the dialed up feelings?

Ideas: _____

_____

What's one thing I can "knock off" that is not serving me?

Ideas: _____

_____

_____

_____

_____

Today? I want to feel productive and connected. I reminded myself that, "What is most important always gets done." Ahhhhhh. I love that. One action that lines up with that thought is to prioritize my list of things to do. I eliminate things that really do not matter, delegate much to my awesome and amazing assistants, and download some new Adele tunes to improve my time. And, lastly, as my southern mama used to say, "KNOCK IT OFF." I decide to stop compulsively checking email, for the sake of my productivity and connection today.

You can use these steps, too. For the next two weeks, use the Dial It Up! Worksheet to practice creating the good-feeling energy states that you want. Try it and notice what happens.

A big part of honoring and nourishing your energy is to connect to the source of it all and listen. I will suggest many things that you can try: kind physical movement, delicious and nutritious fuel foods, even blending up some green smoothie goodness. But, these techniques will be short lived, and you will not be able to make lasting change, if you do not first **learn how to listen to your God, the Universe, your higher self, your soul**. Don't get too hung up on the label here. It's not a religious thing, it's a connection thing.

Texts from God

I hear God talking to me regularly. Do you? If not, or you think I'm crazy, try this little experiment daily and see what happens. Every morning, ask yourself, "If God were to text me right now, what would the text say? What does God most want me to know?"

As a Life Coach, I create all sorts of unusual ways for myself and my clients to *establish a deeper connection* with their God, their higher selves, and listen to their soul's cravings.

I've had clients use this tool to gain quick, unbelievable clarity about some tough issues. So, get off your knees. Stop begging and pleading with God. Start listening.

Area of my life, or issue I would like guidance on: _____

_____

_____

_____

If God, Your Higher Self, the Universe, Your Soul were to *text you right now,* what would it say? (Do not filter your answer or think to hard about this. Go with what pops in your mind.) _____

_____

_____

_____

Ask your *higher power* what it most wants you to know. _____

_____

_____

_____

Then ask yourself, "*Ok, now what?*" How can you take one small step towards living the advice? _____

_____

_____

You can share your inspiring texts at www.TextsFromGod.com

Ideal Life Design
www.ideallifedesign.com

The inspiration for this came from a recent phone coaching session. Kevin is a talented, handsome advertising executive. He's married with one son. From the outside looking in, he's got it all. Behind closed doors, he's having an affair with a co-worker and about to leave his wife. He's tortured with guilt and desperate for connection.

Kevin's mistress texts him six times a day. He said that he loves the sweet messages. He feels loved, excited, treasured when he reads them. The idea came to me in an instant.

"Kevin," I asked. "What would God/Your Higher Self/ Your Soul text you right now? What do you think it most wants you to know?"

"Everything will be ok." And then, tears.

Yes, everything will be ok.

I asked Kevin to write out six text messages from his God, or his soul, or his higher self as homework. This exercise helps Kevin create love and excitement for himself. He's learning that love is an inside job.

Kevin inspired a new coaching tool. It's something that I use with all of my clients and myself now. And, the results are nothing short of powerful miracles.

Here are some of my personal texts from God:

- » You are loved.
- » I am so, so proud of you.
- » You are ready and can do it.
- » This is all for you.
- » Go take a nap, please.
- » It's not as hard as you make it.

- » Everything is always ok.

- » What you are worrying about is a waste of your time.

- » There is no rush. No need to hurry.

- » There's always more when you need it.

- » Sleep is important.

- » On parenting: Compliance is not the goal. Understanding with love and compassion is the goal.

- » One day, you will be as proud as I am of you.

Writing your own text from your God is a really simple shortcut to the truth. I ask myself many times when I am confused or struggling if I were to receive a text from God right now, what would it say? And, 100 percent of the time, I exhale with relief at the answer.

Ridiculous Self Care

After I started doing little things for myself, it motivated me to do more. Eventually, I decided that I was going to be a woman who embodied deep love and care for herself. I vowed that I would make myself No.1 on my "to do" list, and make it my mission to care for myself the same way I cared for my family -- deep, loving, attentive care.

I stepped away from constantly trying to be "better" or "improve myself"and toward love and self-care. There's a difference. It's more about lining up with what's within you, as opposed to pursuing something outside of yourself, to feel better.

"Drop the self-improvement in favor of self-care. It makes me good company. It also reduces the pressure on those around me. Letting go of it all lets me turn my attention to self-care and managing thoughts. Tell you what: life is definitely getting more delicious for me!"
Max Daniels

Hit the pillow. Sleep is important. I received a text from God that said so. So it must be true.

In 2011, the CDC declared the rate of insufficient sleep a public health epidemic. I'm sure you know what I'm talking about. I bet close to half of you reading this are not getting enough sleep. Most adults need between seven to eight hours of sleep. Not getting that? Weight gain, depression, and a weakened immune system are only a few of the consequences.

I've become super diligent about going to bed at the same time each night, and getting at least seven hours of sleep.

Move that body. I was once a professional couch potato. Exercise? Please. I had better things to do, like organize my DVR recordings of "American Idol." In my fast food corrupted brain, I honestly believed that women who worked out were shallow and I had bigger work to do. Well, of course, the only thing getting bigger was my ass. While I was judging healthy people, I was also flogging myself for being lazy.

The benefits of exercise are amazing: mood stabilization; weight loss; lowered risk of diseases such as breast cancer, heart disease, osteoporisis, and a ga-zillion others. Unless you live under a rock, I'm sure you've read all about the benefits of exercise already. The question is why aren't you already doing it? Why wasn't I?

Part of my problem was that I had not yet discovered a form of exercise that I enjoyed. When I made a commitment to self-care for my body, I decided to apply some MIND FUEL creativity to the project. I considered my personality, my lifestyle and my interests. After a while, I found new forms of exercise that I had never tried before that helped me get fit. I've helped others discover activities such as kayaking, hiking, dance, even surfing. Check the Anti-Leotard Campaign and discover something for yourself.

The Anti-Leotard

Exercise Program

When I started the process of connecting with my body and losing weight, I realized that I had a huge amount of resistance to exercise. My vision of exercise was of a 1980's Jane Fonda wannabe strutting through the gym sporting a headband, leg warmers and a shallow ego. I thought that exercise was hard, boring, and took too much of my time to be effective. I discovered many thoughts that were blocking my success. From that "takers" philosophy, I was always doomed to quit.

After examining and replacing my thoughts around exercise, I realized that I didn't have to exercise the way that everyone else did, or stick to someone else's schedule of fitness. I needed to create my own. Here's how I did it.... Come up with traditional exercise that you might like, creative exercise that you will try, consider how you will FEEL when you've completed the exercise, and reward yourself daily and weekly for sticking to your plan.

Develop an Excercise Plan for the Week

Traditional Exercise I might like:
  e.g. group aerobics

How will I feel?
- energized
-
-
-

Creative Exercise I might like:
  e.g. hiking with my kids
  e.g. canoeing with my family

How will I feel?
- happy and energetic
- strong
-
-

Small Daily Reward (non-food): _____

Larger Weekly Reward (non-food): _____

www.ideallifedesign.com

Body Fuel helps your Mind Fuel.

Can you deep fry kale? I was the last person anyone expected to drink kale for breakfast. At 35 pounds overweight, I was addicted to fast food and I never exercised.

I grew up in the South where they deep fry everything. I thought the only greens around were either collard greens cooked with ham fat or iceberg lettuce swimming in ranch dressing. Greens? Yuk. Little did I know then that greens would one day save me from surgery.

As an adult, I convinced myself that I was way too busy raising two kids and juggling a busy career for sanity. I had a Ph.D. in fast food and exhaustion. I was often tired, moody and going through the motions of my life instead of really living it.

In 2008, when I learned how to connect with my neglected body and lose weight permanently without dieting, a whole new world of foods opened up to me. I started to truly understand the connection between processed foods and my energy level, weight, and mood.

I went from fast food twice a day to exploring the delicious world of whole foods. What an education! I re-learned how to cook. I expanded my knowledge of just about everything as it relates to food and the body.

As healthy as I had become, I still found myself gagging down broccoli. I loaded up on fruits and some vegetables, but I still ignored greens.

About a year ago, I started making fruit smoothies with protein powder. My gal pal Jill added kale to her smoothies, so I gave it a try. My nutritionist coach friend Kim Higgins encouraged me to drop a handful of spinach in my smoothies. My Facebook friends started emailing me resources about green smoothies. So, I decided to give it a whirl.

I started adding only a handful of greens to my fruit smoothies. I couldn't taste the greens at all, and felt pretty good about the healthy tweak I had made. In fact, I could almost hear my cells giving me a high five and celebrating.

And then. THEN. Then, I noticed that my skin was crazy soft and smooth. My mid thirties acne was clearing up. My late afternoon crash was virtually non-existent. Huh?

I was pretty sure I had discovered something as world changing as the Internet, Post-its, and sex. You know what I mean. I began reading everything that I could get my eager little hands on about green smoothies.

Why greens? What was so powerful about them? How did they do their magic?

What I noticed next blew my spinach—obsessed mind.

Before I began my obsession with greens, my menstrual cycle had become so heavy that it was interfering with my everyday life. Forget exercise, outings to the beach or hiking with my family during "that time of the month." I was losing so much blood through clotting that it was affecting my activities, my mood and my energy level.

My doctor suggested either bio-identical hormone replacement therapy and/or Endometrial Ablation Surgery. I was digesting these options, and something just didn't seem right for me about them. I was frustrated, and I decided not to do anything about it.

The first month of drinking greens in my smoothies, I noticed that my menstrual cycle was a little lighter. I didn't make the connection until the second month, when my period was two days shorter and the flow was totally normal. The clotting—gone. The PMS symptoms, virtually gone.

Now, I'm pretty much like a TV evangelist about greens, my Vitamix Blender, and using nutrition to improve what physically happens in your body, as well as what happens in your brain.

I can help you blend up some green goodness that doesn't make you want to hurl, and saves you from setting your regular kitchen blender on fire.

You can receive my free e-book on how to make green smoothies at http://ideallifedesign.com/green-smoothies. Just enter your name and email address, and you'll receive a free copy, along with a short video of me making one.

What I've learned is that all of these self-care practices support one another, and make it easier to create change in every realm for sustainable energy.

Chapter 4: Leadership

"There's a fire starting in my heart,
Reaching a fever pitch and it's bringing me out the dark."
Adele, Rolling in the Deep

There's nothing like the smell of horse manure to remind me to stop and check myself. Horses have taught me what I needed to know about my own unique leadership energy, and how to direct and nurture it. Sound crazy? Good. A little crazy is essential in my lucky leadership formula.

One of the easiest things to confuse in the lucky formula is leadership. What I've noticed in coaching hundreds of clients and observing both effective and oppressive leaders is that leadership, when approached with black and white mind crack, can get you managers as dictatorial as the Soup Nazi or as ineffectual as a doormat. If you aren't clear about your own strengths, purpose and direction, you can flip flop between the two styles, and create chaotic life results.

Is leadership dead? I believe that old school leadership through force and "big man on campus" charisma is tired and collecting dust in boardrooms. Author Jeremie Kubinek wrote a book called *Leadership Is Dead*, that illustrates the important point that self-preservation among our leaders has killed their ability to lead and influence. I love how he lays down that the very thing we are afraid of losing, we create through our fear.

Something more is being required of us in leadership today, and it's a completely different vibe. Have you felt it? It sounds like Maya Angelou, looks like a conversation, and feels like warm honey.

Authentic personal leadership -- the warm honey -- will transform you into a luck factory. I've gone from living my life according to everyone else's expectations and road maps, to leading and blazing my own way, based on my values, goals and inspirations. Interestingly, meeting an unbridled horse in the ring taught me more in fifteen minutes about my style of leadership and the deep, strong power within me than all the expensive leadership and team building programs I had suffered through in my adulthood. But more about that later.

I can remember about seven years ago, my family and I were looking for a new home. One was in town with a small city lot, and the other was on the outskirts of town on five acres. We were drawn to both. One, for the 1920s charm and convenient location, and the other for the romantic vision of tons of outdoor space for the kids.

Was I city mouse, or a country mouse? I polled everyone. What do you think? Where would we ultimately be happiest? Could you see me happy in the boonies? Should we buy a John Deer mower? Sound ridiculous? It was. I routinely wrung my hands and made pro and con lists. I hadn't yet learned how to trust my gut instincts, and it was a painful few months. I second-guessed everything, and I wore my friends, family and co-workers OUT. All of my focus was on external validation. After a while, I started to forget whether I was a city or country mouse, and I just felt like a rat.

Back then, I didn't know much about personal leadership. I equated leadership with having a plan or being "large and in charge." But, I had no real understanding of where true inspiration and courage are created. I believed that luck and leadership were random: You were either born a leader, or not.

What I know now is that leadership is less about what you say and what you do, and more about connecting with your own unique blend of awesome. That's right. The more connected you are to yourself, the more you understand what stirs and moves you, the less you need to be concerned with "the art of persuasion" and other bullshit "leadership techniques." When you apply this to your personal life, you stop looking for answers from others, and begin making choices from your deep well of knowing.

As much as I'd like to parlay my ability to direct from my sleep into total world domination (not really), I've discovered that true leadership is less about compliance and more about understanding. Less barking. More humming. And most importantly, to lead others, you must know how to lead yourself. This is not a simple trick. If you think it is, you haven't done it.

This is where horses can teach you a thing or two. You see, horses are very sensitive to what's happening inside of you. They read energy and respond to calm and confidence. Even if you seem outwardly enthusiastic and strong, horses can sense if you are anxious, scattered, worried, angry or unsettled inside. The horse knows. You cannot fool a horse like you can humans. Suits sitting around a conference room table might be impressed by your pulled together appearance or deftness at presentations, but horses? They can smell courage or fear like a strong perfume. And they couldn't care less what brand of boots you're sporting. They are only concerned whether your emotions are pulled together. They care about your connection ability.

It's rather comical to watch humans, donning shiny cowboy boots, march into a horse ring and assume the leadership position. The horse aren't impressed. They either ignore them or run away. A horse only willingly responds to centered, true alignment.

I had the pleasure of learning all about this first hand from Life Coach and Horse Whisperer Koelle Simpson. She's pretty amazing, and her work with horses is profound. When I entered the ring to work with my horse, I was all keyed up, fumbling with my rope, and not sure what to do. I wanted to "get it right." I wanted to become friends with the horse. But, horses do not lie. My inner squirelly-ness sent my horse to the other side of the ring. He was pretty bored and unimpressed. The more I tried to make something happen, the more he just ran around the ring to get away from me. With the help of coaching from Koelle, I learned how to connect with what was going on inside, dial back my intensity, and line up with my river of confidence.

What happened next, I will never forget. The moment I dropped into my core and let go of my mind crack, the horse became interested in playing with me. The second I was willing to leave an agenda behind, I had a four legged creature teaching me in real time how to lead. It was instant feedback.

There I was, in the center of the ring, guiding this gorgeous horse around the ring with nothing more than energy. I learned how to "join up" with my horse. I felt calm and exhilarated at the same time. This was a new feeling combo that I've since learned and have trained my body to notice and remember. This is how it feels to be totally aligned and in the flow.

When a horse accepts its leader, it gives off a series of signs: licking its lips, dipping its head lower to the ground, chewing, its inner ear turned and pointed to listen to you. Once she shows signs of respect, you turn your back to her, face the other way, and let your head and arms drop. This shows the horse you are not threatening her. She will eventually come up to you and put her head on your shoulder and blow on it. Then you should be able to walk around with your joined-up friend, following.

When I noticed my horse bowing his head, and giving me all the signals that he wanted to join up with me, it took some courage to drop everything, turn away and wait for him to follow. When I heard his soft hooves trot over and felt his sweet warm breath on my shoulder, I walked around the ring with the best blessing I had ever received. Yes, he could feel my leadership speak to him, and I recognized a different kind of leader within me. No force, only alignment.

How can this help you with your personal leadership? By aligning with what you want and connecting with your vision, you, too, can become vigilant about noticing and receiving feedback signals in your life.

Remember my pathetic city/country mouse poll? Which was I? I ultimately chose the house in town. We are still here and it's truly a great fit. But, I could have made things so much simpler for myself had I known then how to create an End Game.

Be honest with yourself. Don't filter your answers. Remember, this is for you and your life.

What's Your End Game?

The first step to goal setting is clearly, specifically and positively *stating your goal*. Think about where you want to be six months and one year from now.

Consider what would be ideal in areas of family/relationships, career, physical health, mental strength, and spirituality. Kicking current reality to the curb, with no perceived glass ceiling or pesky Big Mac addiction holding you back, what would your marriage, vocation, appearance, and relationship with God be like for your future self?

Give yourself the space to choose what you want for yourself. Write down your ideas, and create a paragraph or two about the life that you are intentional about living. Be sure to give yourself a deadline, and be specific and positive in the language that you use.

How do I want my *home* to look and feel?

_____

_____

How do I want my *body* to look and feel?

_____

_____

If I was *brave enough*, I would (fill in)…

_____

_____

Example End Game:

By March 2012, I am enrolled in an MBA program, and am on track for a promotion to Regional Manager. I enjoy at least one date night with my husband, and one family night per week. I am committed to jogging four times per week, and am at my ideal weight. I stay connected through church weekly, journaling daily, and taking quiet time for myself each morning.

My End Game:

```



```

Put your end game on three index cards, and carry one with you in your purse, slide one into your car visor, and tape one to your bathroom mirror.

After working on your End Game, do you feel amazing when you read it? Does it make you excited? No? Then, there's still some work to be done. If you feel like it's not quite right, ask yourself the following:

» What am I afraid will happen if I step up and align with who I am?

» What would I do differently if I were not able to worry about this?

» How can I best serve the world using my gifts and talents, and have an amazing time doing it?

» What one new thing can I do today to be more true to who I am?

Unfortunately, most of us only act on these questions when it is life or death. or an emergency. But, I believe our dreams are an emergency of the soul. We must use our flexible, creative minds to develop strategies to make our deepest desires happen.

Scott's Aunt Jane died a few days ago. She was 94 when she passed, and lived a long beautiful life as an independent woman. At her funeral showing yesterday, I couldn't help but wonder as she neared the end of her human existence, if she mentally filed through regrets, or if she drifted away with deep satisfaction. Pictures were lined up of Emily Jane as a baby, a schoolgirl, and a young woman. What were her dreams? Did she go after them? I never asked her.

This year, we've had quite a few family happenings that have pushed me to swim deeper into life's questions about purpose, meaning and passion. My brother-in-law Shawn had a stroke that led to my 100 Day Invitation. (www. ideallifedesign.com/the-100-day-invitation/) His recovery and conviction to be strong and balanced enough to help carry Jane's casket at her funeral are a true testaments to what the human spirit can accomplish.

All this mortality in my face has me considering things. What are the top five regrets people have on their deathbeds?

According to this fantastic article (http://thenextweb.com/
lifehacks/2011/05/31/the-top-5-regrets-people-make-on-their-deathbeds/)
from TNW Lifehacks, the top five regrets at the end of life are:

1. I wish I had the courage to live my life how I wanted, instead of how others expected me to live.

2. I wish that I had worked less, or not so hard.

3. I wish that I had the courage to express my feelings.

4. I wish that I had stayed in touch with my friends.

5. I wish that I had allowed myself to be happier.

These are issues that I coach clients on daily. I listen to the fears and excuses, and help shape shift them into connection, relationships, work that matters, and peace without using food, alcohol, shopping, gossip, or business to self medicate.

Life is too short to substitute what you want with brownies, work, boots or a packed schedule.

» So, I ask you, given your health, genetics, family history, if you had to guess, how old do you think you will be when you pass away?

» How old are you now?

» How many years does that leave for you here on earth?

Let that number sink in. And, now, let's get to work on how you want to spend those years.

If no one would care or object, if money were of no issue, if you had enough time, if you believed you could do it, what would you do with the rest of your life? Would you learn to swim? Travel? Tell THE ONE that you love her desperately? Work less? Brainstorm for 10 minutes. Now, let's set about to do it.

Do not make whiney bullshit excuses. Your soul has no time for baby talk. If you want, go ahead and list all the reasons your mind has alphabetized why you cannot do the things on your list. Go ahead. I'll wait.

Here's what I have to say about your list.

So?

» Pick one thing. ONE thing.

» Create three to five small turtle steps to get it done.

» Coach yourself or get coached around your crappy mind-crack thinking about it. (Use the worksheets from Chapter One.)

Play to Your Edge

Happiness experts have discovered that human beings are actually happiest, and most satisfied, when they are challenged. Content just doesn't cut it. I have found that luck creators are continuously creating opportunities for themselves to "play to the edge" of their capabilities. It's that feeling of doing something just beyond your usual comfort zone, and doing something that is almost too hard for you to do.

Pick one thing/project that you can do this **month** that is *playing to your edge.*

Why did you pick this?

Why is this out of your comfort zone?

What will you gain by doing it?

Pick one thing/project that you can do this **quarter** that is *playing to your edge.*

Why did you pick this?

Why is this out of your comfort zone?

What will you gain by doing it?

What if you didn't wake up?

My brother-in-law Shawn did not wake up last January. He was 38 years old and healthy. A strong runner, an active father of three. Yet, that morning in January, he was unresponsive.

He was transferred via helicopter from one hospital to another. Intubation roused him that day. Tests later revealed he had survived a stroke. His wife, Beth, later joked with him that he wasn't awake for his first helicopter ride.

Have you ever heard a song, read a sign or received some kind of nudge that you knew was a wink from God? I heard the song "Not My Time" by Three Doors Down that afternoon.

> *Cause it's not my time, I'm not going*
> *There's a fear in me and it's not showing*
> *This could be the end of me*
> *And everything I know, ooh, but I won't go*
> *I look ahead to all the plans that we made*
> *And the dreams that we had*
> *I'm in a world that tries to take them away*
> *Oh, but I'm taking them back*

Shawn's not going. It's not his time. He's right here going to rehab. His wife is assembling the right care for him so that he can do his work in the world as an environmentalist, husband, and father. In an instant, their lives changed.

Beth was told that the first 100 days following the stroke were critical to Shawn's rehabilitation. We both respectfully gave the finger to the doctor who suggested that Shawn had ONLY 100 days to regain what he could. So, I joined him. I dedicated those important 100 days to Shawn. He's giving it all he's got. And so am I. Every business decision, every five-mile run, every time I choose love over fear, I am dedicating it in service to Shawn's rehabilitation.

So I ask you, interested reader, will you join us?

Are you living or are you dying? This is the ultimate question. What are you putting off until you are thinner, richer, smarter? What are you delaying until you have more time or until you are ready? Is there something your soul has craved that you've ignored?

Take the next 100 days and let's do something about it. Choose to live. Things can change in an instant.

Line Up Key Areas

Health
Career
Fun/ Play   Spirituality
Relation-ships

Brainstorm these questions as it relates to the *Career* Key Area:

What's working in this area?

_____

_____

_____

_____

What could be better?

_____

_____

_____

_____

What could I create here that is *BRILLIANT?*
List your ideas...

_____

_____

_____

_____

_____

_____

_____

_____

_____

_____

_____

_____

Line Up Key Areas

Career · Health

Spirituality

Fun/ Play · Relation-ships

Brainstorm these questions as it relates to the Health Key Area:

What's working in this area?

What could be better?

What could I create here that is BRILLIANT?
List your ideas...

Line Up Key Areas

Career   Health

Spirituality

Fun/   Relation—
Play   ships

Brainstorm these questions as it relates to the *Spirituality* Key Area:

What's working in this area?

_____
_____
_____
_____
_____

What could be better?

_____
_____
_____
_____
_____

What could I create here that is *BRILLIANT?*
List your ideas...

_____
_____
_____
_____
_____
_____
_____
_____
_____
_____
_____
_____
_____
_____

Line Up Key Areas

Health
Career
Spirituality
Fun/ Play
Relation- ships

Brainstorm these questions as it relates to the *Fun/Play* Key Area:

What's working in this area?

_____
_____
_____
_____
_____

What could be better?

_____
_____
_____
_____
_____

What could I create here that is *BRILLIANT?*
List your ideas...

_____
_____
_____
_____
_____
_____
_____
_____
_____
_____
_____
_____
_____

Ideal Life Design
www.ideallifedesign.com

Line Up Key Areas

Health

Career

Spirituality

Fun/ Play

Relation- ships

Brainstorm these questions as it relates to the *Relationships* Key Area:

What's working in this area?

_____

_____

_____

_____

_____

What could be better?

_____

_____

_____

_____

_____

What could I create here that is *BRILLIANT?*
List your ideas...

_____

_____

_____

_____

_____

_____

_____

_____

_____

_____

_____

_____

_____

Line Up with Your Brilliance

"I'm dropping these bags,
I'm making room for my joy." — I Choose, India Arie

As a luck creator, it's time to let go of whatever is not serving you and your End Game. Go ahead and drop the baggage. You won't need it on this journey. Make note of what you are letting go of, what you are creating for yourself, and sign your commitment to yourself.

What are you dropping?

Old Beliefs: _____

_____

Old Habits: _____

Other: _____

What are you lining up with in these key areas?

Health

Career

Fun/Play   Spirituality

Relation-
ships

That's Brilliant!

Your signature _____   Date _____

Ideal Life Design
www.ideallifedesign.com

Leadership for your life is needed when the tide is high and the water is rough. It's the situations in life that hurt, even burn, that prepare you for something amazing. Just wait. Just watch. You'll see.

Chapter 5: Creativity

"When fire is applied to a stone, it cracks."
Irish Saying

Have you been set on fire? Or experienced the feeling of being "cracked open" by fire and passion through creativity? Far too often, we ignore our fire and it burns out.

It's replaced with obligation and schedules and excuses.

What I've learned in the past few years is that the more creative I allow myself to be, the easier it is to feel the fire, fan the flames, and celebrate the heat. And one of the fastest ways to facilitate hot luck is to tap into your true creative nature.

Growing up, I believed that I wasn't all that creative. In fact, in kindergarten, I just about flunked scissoring. I remember my feisty 5-year-old frustration with all of the rules our teachers enforced around creativity.

Stay within the lines.

Hold it THIS way.

Glue it just like the one we already did for you.

Don't make a mess.

Paint by numbers.

See how nice it looks when you do it this way?

I earned a solid C in coloring throughout early grade school. I couldn't quite color things pretty enough. This didn't sit well with my over achieving must-make-honor-roll self. And, I quickly discounted myself as not creative. Because, unfortunately, creativity is typically billed and sold with titles like painter, sculptor, photographer, illustrator, writer. You know, the arts. But science and math are incredibly creative. My tax accountant? A creative genius (who uses totally legal strategies, I might add, in case you work for the IRS.) My kids, when they really want something, are creativity on steroids.

Real life, practical resourcefulness.

The level of creative thinking my children are capable of is shocking. Shocking! Just ask them to fold the laundry and they will come up with the most creative excuses ever uttered between child and parent. I'm sorry, but having aching fingers from texting too much does not qualify as a legitimate excuse to not fold, but it's creative, nonetheless.

Do You KNOW Where Your Son Is?

When Ryan was almost 11, he wanted to go play with his friends for the afternoon. He often wishes we lived closer to the school where "everyone else lives." Truth be told, we are only about 5 miles from the middle school, but when you want to be included in last-minute pick-up football games and bike rides, that can feel like a million miles. This particular afternoon, I had a coaching session scheduled after school, and was working from my home office. Ryan scribbled me a note that he was going to go outside to ride his bike. I nodded in approval, waved him off and heard him pop the garage open to get his bike and leave. After I finished my call, I realized that he wasn't back from his ride yet, so I went outside to see if I could spot him on our street. No Ryan. I decided that if he weren't back in about a half hour, I would go look for him, as it was nearing dinnertime.

Just as I was about to get in my car and go look for him, the phone rang. Scott was on the other end, half annoyed and half amused. "Do you KNOW where your son is?" My heart sank and my mind raced. Ryan had decided that since mom was busy, he would solve his boredom issue himself. He "borrowed" my GPS out of my car, plugged in three friend's addresses, and pedaled his honey badger (http://youtu.be/4r7wHMg5Yjg only watch if you are not easily offended by potty mouth language) little self across town. Not an easy ride for a 10 year old, and certainly not a safe one. He had to cross some extremely busy intersections, and when the GPS wanted to take him on the expressway, he rode his bike along the highway on side streets. (Don't even get me started on the many different horrifying things that could have happened.) Ryan had a fun time playing in the neighborhood with all of his buddies, until they all had to go inside to do homework and get ready for dinner. Then he realized he was tired and it would soon be dark, so he called his dad to pick him up. Scott agreed to pick him up, only because it was a dangerous route. Otherwise, we would have made him pedal his little rule-breaking self back home! As he sauntered up the front walkway to the front door, I couldn't help but be angry and proud at the same time. Have you ever had that happen? You know that you "should" feel a certain way (The outrage! The horror! A 10 year old who tricked his mom!), but you secretly harbor something else? I was ticked. He he did not ask me if he could go; he took my GPS without permission; and he broke some basic rules we have about where he can ride, how far he can ride, and letting us know where he is going. But I was also proud because he was extraordinarily resourceful. And as a coach, I know this will serve him very well in the world. Ryan had a problem and he solved it with creativity. Mischievious? Sure. But, he had to think about how to solve his problem. No ride? I'll bike there. No directions? I'll look up their addresses in the school directory and use the GPS.

Emily is my child who thrives by expressing herself in the arts, while Ryan is my equally creative child who happens to prefer math, science and football. No matter what talents or interests you ferreted out in Chapter 2, you can use creativity to amp it up and create some luck.

While I am certainly no Hemingway, I've always loved to write. But specifically, I love to write about life. And further, I always really wanted to have a life worth writing about.   I tend to think that I use writing, coaching and living life creatively as my creative expression.

So I was excited to interview the supremely creative Fabeku Fatunmise for this chapter. He describes his vision of creativity and how we can all develop a creative practice to get what we want.

1. **Fabeku, what does Creativity mean to you?**

» Creativity is life!

» The zingy, vital spark that runs through everyone and everything.

» That pulse.

» That rhythm.

» That thing that moves you and feeds you and sets you on fire.

» Creativity is what reminds you that you're alive. It's what brings you home.

» And it has zero to do with what you do.

» It's not about painting or writing or making music.

» That's just how some people express their creativity. But it's bigger than that.

» Creativity is really about how you meet life.

2. **Do you have a regular creative practice, or time that you devote to yourself for creative time? If yes, can you elaborate on what you do, any routine that you have.**

» I'm a sound guy.

» So every day I immerse myself in sound and music.

» Drumming. Gonging. Chanting. Spinning the Ramones full blast

» I start and end every day with some sound-ey something.

» Every. Single. Day.

» No matter how busy I am. No matter how many clients I have. No matter how long my to-do list gets

» Fifteen minutes in the morning. Fifteen minutes at night. Bare minimum.

» That's my practice.

» And, at this point, I'm really devoted to it.

3. What do you notice are the benefits of having creative outlets in your life? How is your business, relationships, inner life enhanced?

» Creativity feeds me.

» It fills me up.

» It keeps my superpowers strong.

» It's like Popeye when he scarfs down some spinach.

» When I'm consistently creative, everything is amped up in the best possible way.

» My intuition is sharper, which helps me and my clients in a thousand ways.

» I have more ideas. And better ideas. Which keeps my business growing and thriving.

» I'm better in my relationships. Because I'm happy and plugged in and energized.

» And I'm better with myself. Totally lined up with who I am and what I'm doing and where I'm going.

» Every area of my life – personal and professional – is better when I use those creative outlets.

» Having a creative practice takes time. But the return on that investment is completely epic.

» I used to feel like I was too busy to be creative. Now I know I'm too busy not to make creativity a priority.

4. **Do you have a personal story about something amazing that resulted from spending time immersed in a creative practice?**

» Something really amazing happened just this week.

» I've had this big project percolating for awhile.

» Scribbling ideas down on index cards. Mind mapping possibilities.

» Constructing frameworks.

» And I had this central metaphor in mind for the project from the start.

» The thing that would tie it all together.

» Except the metaphor wasn't quite right.

» So instead of bringing everything together, stuff started feeling really off. Like I was trying to force the pieces to fit.

» And the more I tried to fix it or think up alternatives, the fuzzier everything got.

» My enthusiasm for the whole project started to wane. The zing had left the building.

» Then, after this fiery fit of drumming, the perfect metaphor just fell into my lap.

» This delivered-by-drumming nugget of aha! brought everything together and filled in all the blanks. It couldn't be more awesome.

» And the zing! It's back!

» A creative practice gives us a way to keep working on things even when we're not doing it consciously.

» And it gets us out of own way so that the aha! can actually show up.

» Which, of course, is half the battle.

5. What advice would you give to someone who wants to amp up their own creativity?

» Find that thing that causes sparks to shoot out of every pore.

» And just do it.

» If you're not sure what that is, that's ok.

» Try a thousand things until you find it.

» Start now.

» Today.

» Do what you can.

» Even if it's only five minutes at a time.

» It matters.

» It will gain momentum.

» And, when it does, don't stop.

» Even when you're busy.

» Even when you feel selfish.

» Even when you're scared.

» Especially when you're scared.

» Keep doing it.

» Day after day. Week after week. Month after month.

» Toss out comparisons and apologies and concessions.

» Protect your creative time.

» Guard it with your life.

» And feed it every chance you get.

6. Fabeku, how can my readers learn more about you?

"I'm Fabeku Fatunmise. (Hi!) Business awesomizer. Suck exorcist. Punk rock alchemist. I help people turn up the awesome in their business + life through the magics of sound. In my spare time, I sip sweet Darjeeling, covet dark chocolate, and write love letters to Yoda. Find me + say hey. I'd love to hear from you.
http://www.sankofasong.com/"

It's time for you to start claiming your own creative practice. Remember, that it's not about necessarily doing something in the arts. But honestly, music, paints, a camera, pen and paper, beautiful surroundings are a great way to tap into your creative genius. For me, there is nothing like a lucky jam (have you downloaded the free Lucky song yet?) to help me live life creatively.

In your memory there is a snapshot of a girl on an
unstoppable mission to invent, create, take risks, and have fun!

~Kathy Vick, Run Like A Girl

We are all creative. Every single one of us. Creativity is something we are born with. You have not been left out. I used to think that I was missing the necessary gene to be a phenom. Only really "gifted" people were creative. I used to think that to be a "creative," I had to be an artist of some sort. A painter, sculpter, photographer. What I know now is that creativity is an approach, not a medium.

The truth is, that living your life is creative. Life is about creating each moment instead of just letting life happen to you. Creativity is making new connections between two things that did not exist before. It's perspective. It's who you are.

Remember when you were little and you would make up games, stories, dances, songs, and plots against authority? All creative. Honor your child-like self. Let's play.

What inspires you? Why?

Top 5 Favorites

Here are some things to revisit to ignite your creativity. List your Top 5 Favorites for each category. Say why they are your favorites. How do you feel when you do a favorite? Where can you get a quick dose of it?

Top 5 Favorite	Why is it favorite?	How do you feel?	Where can you get?
Quotes:			

 Ideal Life Design
www.ideallifedesign.com

Inspiration Junction for Creativity

Top 5 Favorite	Why is it favorite?	How do you feel?	Where can you get?
Movies			
Stores			
Web Sites			
Colors			
Books			
Foods			
Songs			

Top 5 Favorite	Why is it favorite?	How do you feel?	Where can you get?
Scents			
Exercise/Body Movement			
Hobbies			

What commonalities are among your favorites?

_____

_____

_____

Name something new that you view as creative that you are willing to try: _____

_____

_____

Here's what to do with your fabulously inspiring results:

Engage in/with these things a little bit every day. 15 minutes. Watch a YouTube video. Read a few quotes. Exhale. Commit to trying that thing you think is creative this month.

Chapter 6: Fun

Some boys take a beautiful girl
And hide her away from the rest of the world
I want to be the one to walk in the sun
Oh, girls they want to have fun
Oh, girls just want to have fun

-- Cyndi Lauper

Stop all of your fun activities now. Drop 'em like it's hot. I suspect that you might be trying to mani/pedi your way to happiness, and that's merely a recipe for trimmed cuticles and a clipped spirit. I'm not against gorgeous paws. Quite the opposite! I just want to be sure that you've got more going for you than external, purchased fun. You've got to buff and massage your thinking, first.

It's not so much the activity you choose as the attitude and energy you have while doing it. I've been a lonely woman at a fun party and a disconnected one sitting in a mani/pedi chair. In contrast, I've just about had an orgasm creating a business plan, writing emails, or journaling new blog post ideas. None of these activities are typically labeled passionate and sexy. So, what's my secret? Staying connected to who I am, what I want in the present moment, and how I am treating myself in my mind. (MIND CRACK vs. MIND FUEL?)

When I say the word FUN, what comes up for you? Do you get excited? Or do you feel dreadful pressure because you have no idea what is fun anymore?

Way back in Chapter One, we touched on fun, and had a brief tango with the worksheet Becoming Your Own Fun Coordinator on page 52. I hope you've indentified a few things that you've tried and enjoyed. So, what are they? Barrel racing? Hunting mushrooms? There must be something.

Go ahead, exhale.

I've circled back to having fun because it's damn important. I'm just here to gently remind you that you are in charge of whether or not you have fun. Not your mama, your boss or your kids. Fun is a key ingredient to creating luck. It's not dependent on circumstances, money to spend or other people. It's dependent on mind fuel.

Fun connects you with your true nature. It allows you to give more to your circle of influence, and it affects the joy of everyone around you. But fun can also be something just for you. It's your own private buoyancy that can lift you to your personal comedy club.

Most of the time, when I ask people what they do for fun, they cannot tell me. Or, it takes them a long while to consider it before they come up with something tantalizing like, "We go to dinner and a movie sometimes." Lame. I know there's more for you than that.

I like to have fun for a living, but even my favorite fun activities can get worn out with repeat business. I recently visited my favorite online fun place, Facebook, to ask my people what they do for fun. It was truly FUN to read everyone's ideas. There were some common threads, and fresh twists to some tried-and-true favorites.

Get your highlighter out because you are going to want to try as many of these as you can, ASAP!

"A FUN day is when you have the WHOLE house to yourself and you play 80s music as loud as you can and dance like you're 25 again!"

Teri Proffitt

"Teaching the kids to fish in our lake."

Danielle Erley

"Fun for me is quality time with my family...doesn't matter what we're doing as long as we're doing it together. Doesn't get any better than that!! We love Friday night football games, family movie night, roasting hotdogs over our bonfire, family vacations, and just sitting around being silly together!"

Kelli Seaton

"A good old fashioned game of whiffle ball in the back yard with our teen boys and whoever else would like to play!"

Pamela Dravicszki

"DANCE! Sometimes my hubby and I create a mini-playlist - we each pick two or three songs - and we just dance like fools in the living room. Not cool dancing. I'm talking free—spirited, childlike, wild abandon dancing. It usually ends with us completely out of breath, lying on the floor together and laughing. GOOD STUFF."

Joy Tanksley

"Camp fire on the beach, drums, conversation, dancing, skinny dipping and laughing. Waking up there because no one wanted to leave."

Anthony Bouoard

"What else? Dance party! At home, with the kids. When all else fails and I'm about to lose my effing mind, I drop everything and crank the tunes. No more yelling, no more whining, just dance."

Andrea Owen

"Hang out with my neighborhood friends, watch my kids run wild with their friends in the hood, go to book club, hang out with my bestie, go to Ignite Fort Collins (a local mini-TED) with my hubby on date night, write books, take kickboxing."

Tracee Sioux

"When I drive long distances, I put my seat back so I can sit up, (Yes, I'm driving), turn on my playlist called SONGS I LOVE really really loud and dance! YES, you can dance sitting down without endangering yours or your fellow travelers lives!"

Kelly Pratt

Kitty wrestling. Painting. Gonging my face off. Wearing red shoes. Or monkey slippers. Or pretend I'm walking a runway. Endless possibilities."

Fabeku Fatunmise

"We have Backwards Friday. When the kids get home from school, we pick our treat (ice cream, cinnamon buns, or s'mores, etc.) then we head out to have dessert before supper. We savor every single bite. Then we go pick a movie, head home, get our PJs on, then cook breakfast for dinner (pancakes, waffles, or eggs etc). Then we get all the blankets and pillows we can find and watch the movie all snuggled together on the floor!! So FUN. I'm sure I love it more than the kids do."

Gaynor Levisky

"I love Halloween camping! It is so FUN. We go with a big group of friends and all of their kids, more kids than adults! The kids run free for the weekend, riding their bikes everywhere. They're like The Little Rascals. The adults, while doing all the work around camp, enjoy some free time together. Yes, there are gross parts, what with the nasty toilets, and the no bathing for 3 days, but the pay off is great. The kids love the Saturday afternoon costume parade and trick-or-treating!"

Kelly Johnson

"We love to sit on Tybee Island and play bocce ball, and going to our boys little league games."

Lori Barlow

"I go into my garden or to the park and observe Nature. Nature provides some of the funniest shows ever! Animal fights, courtships, attempts at doing or achieving something (especially trying to get nuts, fruit and paper or plastic bags to open, rip or crack so they can access the food inside), territorial displays, parenting lessons... you name it! Nature provides it! And then, of course, I watch humans... 'nough said!"

Pedro Baez

"Playing at the park. (You're never too old for the slide or the swings.) And spinning the kids on the merry-go-round until they can't stand up :) Then we all lay on the ground and giggle."

Sabrina Holden

"We geo—cache. http://www.geocaching.com/ It gets everybody hiking with a goal in mind ("Let's find the hidden treasure.") and the kids don't even realize how far we're going!"

Heidi Loren

"I gather my favorite people and orchestrate activities, food and LIVE laugh-out-loud moments. So much fun! My second favorite thing is watching and/ or playing with animals, dogs, cats, birds, whales. Any shape or size will do. This makes me smile ear to ear!"

Valerie Steiger

"Taking mini-vacations with my kids on the weekends! We love to take road trips to towns we've never been to and see what we can find. We love to try their local restaurants and find souvenirs that represent the town. We go to big cities and towns with no traffic lights. It's always a fun adventure!"

Rhonda Gassman

"We get cooking: baking cookies; rolling pasta; grinding spices for an Indian feast. Never-fail fun. Popcorn under the stars with big duvets is a different, dreamier kind of fun."

Tanya Geisler

"Hop into the kitchen — and bake! We are suckers for Banana bread. Fall means pumpkin bread. And I love to step out on a limb and try something exciting like scones, or dig into the current season and bake a fruit crumble."

Deb Smouse

"Drumming on the beach under full moon, ocean swimming at dusk, dancing in the rain!"

Jen Beckman

"I have a lot of fun getting realtors to show me ocean front homes that I'd love to live in. Pure magic."

Linda Ford

Yucking it up with someone in person or over the phone. Fantastic fun!"

Maria Dolson-Verroye

"I totally get in touch with the 10-year-old part of myself when we go to an amusement park. My husband and I started an annual tradition of taking our daughter to a regional park (like Holiday World or King's Island) the week before school starts and riding everything we can fit into a day. It is so much fun to ride roller coasters with her and laugh and scream our heads off. It's fun for me to watch other people my age and older do the same, and let that inner kids out. I love that goofy, disheveled, uninhibited, happy and hilarious look we all share as the ride ends and we're rolling back in to let the next group get on."

Laura Wagner

"I like to cook Italian food and play Andrea Bocelli so loud that I can sing my heart out to the Italian lyrics in my kitchen and sound fantastic! PS - I'm a terrible singer. As in, even in church I just mouth the words."

Gretchen Pisano

"Think about all things ridiculous."

Sarah Bamford Seidelmann

"Sing, sing, sing! I'll find a song and learn it inside and out. Or throw a karaoke party. I love to see what songs people will pick. It is fun to see everyone really cut loose. I really enjoy gathering people at our house to eat, drink and hang out. Especially if it is a weekend and we can fire up Rock Band on the X—box! Are you seeing a theme here?"

Elise Touchette

"Our fun family tradition is Disney. For the past 18 years, we have been to Disney World in Florida. I believe we have become so accustomed to it that we are considered 'experts' when it comes to Mickey. We are also a tennis family, so while we are there we get to play tennis with the 'stars'. We have 18 years of autographs (from the Disney characters), tennis balls signed by the pros and video to prove it (Actually, it started on VHS tapes and then to mini 8 tapes, and now on DVDs)."

David Wu

I draw with sidewalk chalk, much to the mortification of my 11-year-old son. I write quotes, I sketch out symbols, but mostly, I draw rainbows, stars, trees, flowers, the unrecognizable animal or two. This makes me ridiculously happy, as does watching everyone who walks by slow down to look and smile. One woman even took a cell phone picture! I thought she was the HOA police, but turned out she just thought my doodles were cool. The other thing I really love to do is drive my car really fast while playing songs I really can't sing but do, anyway, at the top of my lungs."

Maggie Laura McReynolds

"We quote memorable movie lines with our 9 year old son in public places. No one else knows what we are talking about and we laugh our heads off. If someone DOES recognize the quote, it's even funnier!"

Lisa Benesh

"Family dance party, laughter with loved ones, Saturday afternoon grass volleyball with a great group of friends for the past 9 years, jumping on the trampoline with the boys, all things connected with nature (this list about nature feels endless and starts with a round pen and a horse), and driving hubby's Lotus Elise FAST around a race track!"

Diane Hunter

"Jewelry beading while having the TV in the background (funny reruns, especially). This is very calming, relaxing and fun, especially when I see the finished jewelry."

Maria Frias

"I have fun tending my garden, walking my dog, being silly with my daughter (who really gets me), talking with girl friends and laughing about life, laughing at sitcoms. The more silly I can let myself be the better."

Gail Kenney

"Running. And hanging out with my family in the backyard playing cards and chatting. Or having friends over for a glass of wine. Flashlight tag in the backyard with the whole family."

Frances Cadora

"These things never get old: 1. Telling painfully bad jokes and then asking my husband 'On a scale of 1 to funny, how funny do you think I am?' This makes me laugh hysterically every single time. Also, butt humor."

Sarah Yost

"I act as silly as I want to act. So silly that if I was seen doing half the things in public, I would probably be taken in for testing at an institution."

Meghan Currie

"I celebrate obscure holidays. Examples: National Ice Cream Cone day; Talk Like a Pirate Day; Sweetest Day (That's how I snagged my hubby.); Count Your Buttons Day."

Kanesha Baynard

"Playing with my golden retrievers; dancing to almost any music - but zydeco and rock'n'roll most of all; creating, in one way or another; reveling in color; reconnecting to activities I loved to do as a child."

Laurie Hawley

"We cast co-workers in the movie of our college, using real actors living or dead who capture the essence of each person --not necessarily on looks alone. Once you start this your mind loves it!"

Beth Herman

"For fun I read some transformative, right brain, life altering words, share the info with a friend and discuss the AHAs. Okay and maybe drink a little wine in there, too."

Danette Butler

"Taking spontaneous road trips; jumping in puddles in the rain; singing as I push my daughter in the shopping cart around the grocery store; opening any cookbook, selecting a random page and making whatever it is for dinner."

Patricia Neal

"Make a snowman and or drive around and take pictures of other kids snowmen. They are all so unique!"

Debby Werthman

"Making up a dance move I've never done before."

Rose Regier

"The best thing in life is Friday night in the fall: high school football. Your stomach in knots because you are so nervous for your boy(s); the smell of the grill cooking hamburgers and hot dogs; the band warming up so they can help get the crowd into yet another wildly exciting close football game. Every year when I start feeling fall in the air, I get so excited because to me, Football season is the closest thing to Heaven there is out there!"

Jennifer Young

What's your flavor of fun? Let's borrow the attitude and mind fuel of Paulo Coelho, "A philosophy of life: I'm an adventurer, looking for treasure." Your life, your fun, is an adventure. So, determine your sweet spot convergence of fun thinking, playful energy and real life goodness.

» Did anything tug at your true self while you read through the fun suggestions?

» Be sure to highlight the ideas that jumped out at you, or write new ideas in the margins.

» What was fun for you as a kid? Is there a grown up version of that? Just because you are grown up doesn't mean that you can't play flashlight tag, or jump in rain puddles, or bring back the wonder, curiosity and excitement that you had as a child into your daily experience.

» What have you been dying to try, but have told yourself you do not have the time, money or ability to do it?

» Is there an opportunity for restorative fun?

Live your fun. Because life is too delicious to rely on Netflix and fast food. Word.

Chapter 7: Vision

"The empires of the future are empires of the mind."
Winston Churchill

Excuse me hon, but there's some sucky vision between your two front teeth. It takes a good friend to tell you to grab some floss, but it takes an even better friend or family member to nudge you to take a look at your life's results. In Chapter 1, I mentioned that my mom whipped out some "southern ninja" action and suggested that I take a break and look at why I was so overwhelmed. Thank goodness she did. It was truly a pivotal moment that began a luck creation process.

Whatever you are experiencing right now -- your bank account, your scale weight, your career, your relationships – is the result of your vision. You created your vision with either mind fuel or mind crack. Don't like it? Let's use some vision floss.

We are raised to stay within the lines. But, color-by-numbers living doesn't require vision. It actually requires the opposite. Living between the lines requires you to put your blinders up, hide behind the status quo, and squash any glimmer that you might have for lucky living. Go to school, get a degree, get a job, get married, have some kids, keep up with the Joneses. Blah.

On the other hand, it's not nearly enough to just dream. It's fun, and it can feel exciting to dive into the possibilities. But it's tempting to just stay there. The steps in this book build on one another to create vision. I've read other books that suggest you trot out with vision first, but I've highlighted it last. And here's why: creating your own luck is impossible without clarity; it's hard without leadership mojo; it's difficult without passion and energy; and there's zero enjoyment without creativity and fun involved.

I was lucky to get my friend Pam Slim, author of *Escape From Cubicle Nation*, to answer some interview questions for us about how to create and implement life vision. Do you need to thaw your soul? Read on and find out!

1. **You are someone who I consider to be a VISION architect. What's the first thing you encourage your clients to consider when they think that they "have no vision?"**

   » *If my clients feel they have no vision, it is often because they need to thaw their souls. People who have been in unhappy work situations, difficult personal relationships or living with high levels of stress are often out of touch with their true voice and creative muse. So I recommend that they do things like sleep, then go to places that bring them great creative joy, like a beautiful hiking trail or an uplifting museum. By feeding their souls with things that make them happy, their visions start to return, and they are ready to imagine what a better future may look like.*

I love the phrase "thaw their soul." If you feel like you do need some thawing, revisit the worksheets from Chapter 3 on Ridiculous Self Care, or Chapter 5 on Fun.

2. **Why is having a VISION for one's life important?**

   » *A vision for your life has three major benefits: it helps keep you motivated, it helps you make decisions and it makes it much easier to get more of what you want. If you go through life making decisions based on only what is in front of you, you will contribute a fraction of what you are capable of to the world. We understand this when we look at huge personal visions, like Martin Luther King's dream of racial equality, but also in smaller ways by noticing which students are most effective securing scholarships for college. When you know what you are driving at in the long run, you will make small progress each day that adds up to very powerful long-term impact.*

This is an amazing point that Pam has made. It's truly the difference between living in reaction mode vs. creation mode. If we power through the day and constantly react to what is happening, we rob ourselves of our ability to rise up above the present circumstances to see the horizon. The big picture.

3. Do you have any suggestions for people who have a dream or vision, and are not sure how to "make it happen."

» *The best way to bring a vision alive is to deconstruct it. If you want to have your own television show on Oprah's network, ask yourself: "What are the specific skills, experience, resources, expertise, connections and reputation that I need to have my own show on OWN?" If you don't know, then find out! With this long list of things you need to accomplish, work backwards from your projected "vision accomplished" date and work on a small piece at a time.*

That first sentence is so good it makes my head want to explode. In a good way, people! Bring your vision alive by deconstructing it. Can I get an Amen? Get resourceful. What do you need? What do you need to learn? Get educated. Who can help you find the answers and connections?

4. What do you suspect is the biggest obstacle to creating a VISION for one's personal life? Is there something that you've observed as a common "hiccup" for clients?

» *The biggest obstacle to creating a powerful vision is a grumpy committee of naysayers in your own head. You start with "I would REALLY love to own a house on the beach in Hawaii!" Immediately, voices pop up that say "But that is ridiculously expensive! Where are you going to get money for that, on your current salary as a bike messenger?" At the brainstorming and vision creating stage of the game, you do not want to rule out anything. If you don't allow yourself to imagine what you want for long enough to do a real test in the real world, you will never make big moves happen.*

So true! Mind Crack takes so many forms, and listening to a stadium of haters is a fast road to *iwasalwaysgonnadothat* 'ville. If you notice that your mind is filled with voices drunk on *haterade*, revisit the Mind Crack/Mind Fuel exercises. You deserve to listen to empowerment. Tune in.

5. **What would you say to someone who is frustrated that they have not been able to see their VISION come to fruition?**

» *Three things: check your expectations, analyze your methods and revisit your vision. I frequently meet people who are frustrated that they have not gotten the same results as someone who has been plugging away for years longer than they have. Doing epic things and making progress requires time. Many people give up right as they are gaining momentum toward accomplishing their goals.*

» *Other times, their vision doesn't come to fruition because they have been utilizing methods that don't work. Look at examples of people who have had success, and pay close attention to what they did. You may begin to notice patterns of particular strategies or methodologies that have a better chance of success than the ones you have been using.*

» *Finally, sometimes your vision changes. If you are working toward something and never seem to get anywhere, perhaps it is not the right thing, or the right time. It is OK to give up one dream to make room for a new one.*

6. **Do you have a favorite inspirational story about a client that you can share that demonstrates a unique and powerful VISION?**

» *One of my clients, Amanda Wang, has a mental illness called Borderline Personality Disorder, or BPD. The characteristics of this illness are low self-esteem, mood swings and frequent thoughts of self-injury. Amanda struggled deeply with her BPD until she was diagnosed, and then treated by a therapist that brought much relief. Amanda decided to train for the Golden Gloves, and to make a documentary of her experience called The Fight Within Us, which draws parallels with the challenges of boxing, and the challenges of living with BPD on a daily basis. She writes articles and speaks to physicians, therapists, patients and family members of people with BPD to provide education and inspiration. She struggles with her illness on a daily basis, but has such a strong vision of how she wants to help those in her community, that she moves forward despite the challenges. I am enormously humbled to watch what she accomplishes while she fights deep doubts on a daily basis.*

What an amazing example Amanda is for all of us. She's creating her own luck despite a mental illness, and using it to also empower and help others.

"If you limit your choices only to what seems possible or reasonable, you disconnect yourself from what you truly want, and all that is left is a compromise."
— Robert Fritz

Real vision is seeing the future with your spirit, through your body, in a way that tastes delicious to the senses. For me, I know I'm on the right track when my body exhales, my mind is excited, and gut says YES!

But remember that your mistakes, fumbles, and epic fails are all channeling your brilliance. Pay attention to them. Consider them the building blocks of your vision. They can provide clues for your next steps. Many times, what we are afraid of is exactly where our soul must go.

I've never been much of sports athlete. In fact, up until about three years ago, I believed a lot of the messages I received growing up that I was just not coordinated. Not an athlete. At all. I didn't ride a bike on two wheels until I was ten years old. I couldn't run and dribble a ball at the same time. I was a really enthusiastic bench warmer.

To my surprise, after being willing to look like a complete fool, I followed my feel good and became a runner. An athlete who completes half marathons. Who runs five miles a day, four times a week, because I just don't feel good if I don't. It's kind of badass. It's so fun for me that it led to me becoming a road cyclist, as well. The little girl who couldn't ride without training wheels, now straps on a helmet, clicks shoes into her pedals, and sometimes rides 30 miles at a time.

When I spent all of those hours at team sport practices, wishing I as more talented at hoops, or the volleyball net, or home plate, what I didn't know was that what I craved, I could create. I really can't do a lay up, or hit a home run, or spike a volleyball. But I have endurance, I can run, I can bike, and I can cross a finish line. That's what I was craving. There's something really amazing about developing the mental strength to finish strong.

Like my friend Pam Slim so beautifully articulated, it's important to toggle between rising up and seeing the big picture, and taking small steps in the here and now to get things done. I hope you've got your End Game from Chapter 4 plastered everywhere you might see it. But there's something that I learned about myself watching my son Ryan's last football game that I think is essential to bringing vision to life.

Warning, this is the part where the woman who knows almost nothing about team sports and Football, is going to trot out some Football coaching advice for life vision. If you are knowledgeable about the game of football, my husband Scott tells me that you will most likely disagree with me, like he did, quite heatedly, sitting in the stadium bleachers last week. But this honey badger don't care.

Ryan plays middle school football for the 7th grade team. He's a pretty incredible middle line backer, and obviously inherited some hand-eye coordination from someone other than me. I'm pretty stoked he's found an outlet for all of his badassery.

The game was a close one. His team played hard and they were losing by two points. The winning team drove the ball down the field, but Ryan's mighty defense held them on the SIX INCH YARD LINE. You read that right. With ten seconds left on the board, the offense decided to stand there and run out the clock. Six inches from the end zone. Six inches from another touch down. The defensive line stood there deflated. They were not going to get the chance to do another play. The clock ran out. The winning team ensured their win and walked off the field. It was like someone sucked all the energy out of the stadium.

I was BESIDE MYSELF.

What? They aren't even going to TRY?! I shouted. Why wouldn't the opposing team's coach run a play? Why would they DO THAT with time on the clock and only SIX INCHES to go? They were so close. Scott Hyatt patiently explained that it was a smart move on the coach's part. What if they fumbled? And we recovered the ball? They could blow the whole game. They needed to run the clock out to ensure their win.

I have a problem with this.

The vision cannot be just to "win." Success cannot be the only goal. Although my husband assures me that in the strategic game of football, that is absolutely the goal. Win. It's a competitive sport. Scott argued that the coach was actually teaching the kids the strategy of the game.

Here's the thing. I want to be on the team that has the courage to go for it. Every damn time. Forget the fear that they might fumble. They might fumble? Is that how a team should make decisions? I want to be on the team that says, the pressure is on, the stakes are high, but let's go the extra six inches. Let's see what we can do.

I want to be on the team that plays when there is still time on the clock. Fear of fumbling is a pretty lame strategy, in my humble opinion.

So, my friends, you are on the six-inch yard line. Rise up and look at the big picture. Your vision has time on the clock. What kind of strategy does YOUR team have? Fear of the fumble, or anticipation of a score?

I'll give you a high five in the end zone. I'm there waiting for you. Go get your lucky on.

It's Just the Beginning

"Go on shake it up, what you gotta lose?
Go and make your luck with the life you choose
If you want it all, lay it on the line
It's the only life you got, so you gotta live it big time"
Big Time Rush

I am really proud of you. By reading this book, you are showing yourself that you matter. Your life is important. Your experience should be a celebration, and the fun that you are meant to have is absolutely critical. I am as serious as a heart attack.

You need to be having so much fun that people talk; you need to feel so full of gratitude that you well up with tears; you need to connect with such depth that you develop a knowing that eradicates anxiety; and you need to create with such passion that people will sigh and marvel at "just how lucky" you are.

But you'll know the truth. You created it.

But, reading this book and letting it sit idle on your desk is not enough. Creating luck starts with talking about the lucky concepts with your friends. Then, you actually have to do the exercises. That's what speeds things up. If you want more luck, it's all there. It's always been there.

The No. 1 thing that lucky people have in common is a positive mindset. There's no other shortcut to lucky living. It takes changing mind crack to mind fuel. If you do nothing else after reading this book, at least devote yourself to understanding the process of changing the way that you think.

Birds of a feather flock together. Yep. Hang with other lucky people. Find a lucky role model, mentor or coach. Coaching myself, and getting coached, is something that I invest in because it works. It keeps me lucky.

And please, do me a big favor. Honor what you want. Follow your own gut. Let the naysayers have their opinions. And spend your energy on the things that lift you up.

The life you want to create is already in motion. As you read these words, you are creating it. This is your sign, and right now is your moment.

Your lucky life is calling. Claim it.

- Bonus Readings -

Best of Susan's Blog for even more luck

Do The Potter . . .

It seems like inspiration is everywhere when you look for it. Consider my latest source of joy, Harry Potter. I haven't even seen the new movie, only the previews, and was moved to tears. My 9-year-old daughter Emily thought this was rather amusing as I passed the popcorn.

What struck me as so awesome while I watched the preview of Harry Potter was a line that might not impress a lot of people. But, I felt that what he said was so brilliant and clear, I had to share it. In the trailer, Harry is trying to rally the other witch and wizard students to help him fight the newest dark enemy. Everyone is afraid and protesting that it's impossible to do it. And Harry, in all of his Hollywood glory says, "All truly great wizards started as nothing more than we are now. If they can do it, why not US?!" (Or something very similar. I was so knocked over that I could be hallucinating.)

What that statement means is that everyone who is accomplished, enlightened, famous, notorious, self-made, etc., all started somewhere. And more often than not, they started on their quest against major obstacles. As a coach, I encourage my clients to imagine, "What if?" What if I COULD go back to college and become a teacher. What if I did take a risk and open my own business? What would it be like to try and run a marathon? As humans, we come up with all sorts of interesting excuses why what we profess to be our greatest wish is impossible. I can't go back to school because I don't have the money. Who am I to think that I could open my own business? Running a marathon would be too hard. My answers: student loan, who are you NOT to open your own business, and so what? I realize that I am simplifying, but you get the picture. You have to start saying SO WHAT to welcome what might be so. (Someone really cool said that, but I can't remember who.).

I am currently working on two books. Occasionally, I'll fall into the trap of listening to some self limiting thoughts like, "Who do you think YOU are to write a book?" But, you know? Who am I not to? I have a lot to say. Ha-ha!

I am going to "Practice the Potter" and realize that all great authors, before they wrote their first book, sat in front of a blank page or computer screen and took it one word at a time.

Over the next week, notice when you are putting up your own road blocks. Observe your thoughts and challenge them. They are only thoughts, and you can choose them. Ask yourself, "Who would I be without that thought?" If Harry Potter used his magic wand to eliminate the thought, "I will never be a writer," how would my day/week/year/life be different?

I'd be slaying chapters, dude!

What can we learn from Walt Disney

My family just returned from a week long vacation to Walt Disney World. It was great practice for me to choose my attitude and experience among the two-hour lines for one-minute rides, and capitalism (which I typically embrace) at its peak. Really, how many stuffed Mickey and Minnie animals can one own? According to my daughter, Emily, you can't own too many.

While I tend to find "magical" experiences more likely at the lake, watching the sun create pink hues across an unencumbered shore line, and at a more relaxed pace, I chose to have fun. I think we often forget that everything in life is a choice. You can create what you want by simply adjusting your thoughts and feelings. So, while shelling out extraordinary amounts of money for Disney collectible trading pins, sweatshirts and post cards, I experienced some "Disney Magic," just as Walt Disney must have intended. No, it didn't come as a result of having an exclusive breakfast at Cinderella's Castle, or even from being chosen as part of Disney's "Year of a Million Dreams" to be in the Animal Kingdom parade (I am not making this up.) When I chose to ignore what I didn't like, and focused on what was really cool, I felt like the late Walt Disney was speaking to me personally:

"When you believe in your dreams, you can do it. Always remember that this whole thing was started with a dream and a mouse."

"It's kind of fun to do the impossible."

"KEEP MOVING FORWARD."

These are just a few of the positive and really spectacular messages sprinkled throughout the park (like Tinkerbell's fairy dust), parades, movies and rides at Disney World. I chose to embrace and highlight those for my family while I slurped down a $6.99 Icee, waiting for a late shuttle bus. HA!

Freedom From Fear

The boogie man. Applying for a job promotion. Nuclear War. Going back to school. Your mom's meat loaf. It doesn't matter what the fear is, if it keeps you from becoming more of who you want to be, then it's time to face it.

In Embracing Fear, author and therapist Thom Rutledge identifies two types of fear, your ally and bully. Fear can be an ally. It is a biological protective mechanism that is an instinctual response to danger. Steering clear of the neighborhood pit bull that enjoys snacking on ankles is a good example of healthy fear at work.

However, authentic fear's ugly cousins, anxiety and worry, serve no practical purpose and "bully" us from successfully living our lives. Like when you skipped the company pool party because of anxiety about publicly wearing a swim suit. Or, when you didn't apply to college, even though you wanted to become a dentist, because you were afraid you would never make it.

Is fearless living possible? How can we approach the invisible, yet, powerful kryptonite in our minds? Will mom ever leave gross leftovers out of her meatloaf?

Fight or Flight

The fastest way to determine if what you are facing is something to run from (like the pit bull) or stay with (like applying to school), is to ask yourself what you want. We want what we want, even in the company of fear. If your fear and desire are both communicating the same thing, flee. But, if you experience fear, and you really want that something anyway, fight. For example, you really want to participate in a triathlon but are scared that your swimming will not be up to par. Face your fear and learn how to do it anyway.

Just Do It

Nike's genius marketing aside, they're onto something here. When we allow ourselves to feel the fear, and muster the courage to do it anyway, we find freedom.

When we face what frightens us, we learn what we need to do to fulfill our desires. Perhaps we need to begin triathlon training, or hire a swimming coach. Fill in the blank: If I were brave enough, I would _____. Join the military? Take a class? Eat the meatloaf? Just do it.

Stink At It

What? Be willing to stink at it. Many of us sit on the sidelines because we fear we will not be able to do it perfectly, or even "good enough." The only way to become better at anything is to make mistakes, fail, get back up, and try again. So much time is invested in how we appear to others that we miss out on life. Be willing to be terrible at something, to look like a fool, to gag on the meatloaf.

Many of us hang out on the sidelines of life, safe yet unfulfilled. The famous line from Eleanor Roosevelt, "Do something that scares you everyday," is the mantra of how to turn fear into freedom. Evaluate what is stalling your progress. Step outside of your comfort zone and take some risks. Decide that your goals, your one life, is more important than yielding to fear. Choose courage. Enjoy freedom.

Make Your Own Luck Part 1

If you feel that you are a resident of Bad Fortune, there's actually new research to back up what I've been telling clients forever: Luck has nothing to do with success. That's right. Some guys do NOT have all the luck. What they have instead is the ability to THINK and ACT in a way that gets them the results that they want in life. So brush that chip off of your shoulder and listen up. You can make your own luck.

"He's just lucky. He can come out of a pile of manure smelling like a bed of roses. It's been that way his whole life," a family member commented about my husband, Scott. Knowing what I know about his life, he does seem to have "nine lives." But does successfully overcoming many serious traumas and situations make someone lucky? What exactly makes a former partier, terrible student, and chronic rule breaker (a.k.a., mother's worst nightmare) into an amazing partner, fun dad and wildly successful professional? I'm not about to hand his power over to a four-leaf clover or being born under a lucky star.

According to my observations, and psychologist and author of The Luck Factor: Changing Your Luck, Changing Your Life: The Four Essential Principles, Richard Wiseman, it's not dumb luck.

It's the ability to see what is possible and being open to new opportunities.

Of course, the self-help industry has been saying this for years. Positive thinking isn't just squishy, woo-woo concepts that only tree-hugging, Birkenstock-wearing, organic-food-eating, New-Age peeps can do. Okay, I am fully embracing that I love trees and eat organic…but I draw the line at ugly shoes. Seriously, my conservative, Midwestern, four wheeling husband gets this stuff, and you can too.

Here's how to be lucky:

1. **Be open for opportunities.** I believe that we are presented with many opportunities every single day. If we start to notice, and become Scientists in our own lives, we begin to see the connections that exist for us. Let your guard down. Talk to people. Be the watcher. Notice all of the unexpected things that are happening for you, and not against you.

2. **Listen to your gut.** Our society spends way too much time relying on our cluttered, hyper minds. What's interesting is that our gut instincts are often way more accurate than the pro/con lists that we create from our minds. Sure, the mind and body have to work together. But often we ignore the body all together. While you are watching for opportunity, also pay attention to your body's signals. I'm sure you can remember a time when your gut said "This isn't a good idea," and you did it anyway, only to regret it? Me too. You body is a great tool that is free and always with you. Pay attention to what it has to say.

3. **Think lucky thoughts.** I'm not suggesting ridiculous mantras that you do not believe. Pick something that you believe that also feels better than your current thought patterns. For example, "The company received 2,000 applications for the same job. The economy stinks and I'll never find a job," probably feels pretty crappy and will lead to some crappy result. The "lucky" person who landed the job was not thinking like this, I can promise you. Replacing that thought with something like, "I am SO qualified for this job and I will rock the interview," is bound to get a different and better result.

4. **Do what the lucky do.** Based on thinking better feeling thoughts, you will FEEL better, which will cause you to ACT in a way that will lead to the result that you want. Ask yourself what you want, then figure out what you need to THINK and DO to get that result. This is how the lucky get luckier, the rich get richer, the happy get happier, and my beagles get more than their fair share of beef jerky.

Scott is a great example of what is possible. He's had plenty of life tragedy and heartache. He learned early on how to change his thoughts and his actions to get results. He does not let life happen to him. He creates his luck. And I am damn lucky to have him!

Make Your Own Luck Part 2

What do a recent concussion, losing power at the house for four days, a car accident, losing my voice, and many other minor happenings have in common? A really lucky person. I recently blogged about the research of luck, and how to get lucky yourself. Soon after, I slipped and hit my head so hard on a car door mirror, that I had a concussion. A client emailed me and asked when the locusts were coming. I laughed. This is no Book of Job.

What's funny is that if you look at the past six months, I've had quite a few inconveniences. But I am still lucky. I feel lucky. And, more interestingly, I realize that many people would use those same life circumstances to have a pity party, and claim that they are UNLUCKY. Just take the concussion for example: Did I love the fact that I had a goose egg on my head, was so exhausted that I had to clear my coaching schedule for a week, and was forced to actually rest? No.

But I took that smack on the head very metaphorically. I should rest more. I move so fast that sometimes I don't notice where I am going. I got the message. It was actually the best thing that could have happened for me to reconnect with myself and self-care.

Notice what I just did? I retold my past in a way that was empowering for me, instead of wallowing in self-pity ick. Self-care or self-pity? Your choice. And, now, your turn.

Here's how to turn your ancient history into a good luck charm:

1. Think about a life circumstance that was unwanted and painful.
2. How was that circumstance PERFECT for you at the time?
3. How does that experience and knowledge help you now?
4. What did that eventually lead to that is good and right in your life?

From this place of empowerment in the present moment, you can let your past off the hook, and create a future filled with luck. It's not just for the Irish. Happy St. Patty's Day.

Girl Interrupted

There's an insane patient in your head and she needs a nap.

I am being very serious.

Are you listening to what you are telling yourself? Have you eavesdropped on the crazy conversation in your head? If you do not have what you want in your life, I guarantee that your thoughts are sabotaging what you say you want.

Just yesterday I was coaching a bright, energetic, lovely client who says that she wants to lose 50 pounds more than anything. But, when I asked her if she believed that she was capable of actually losing the weight, she meekly replied, "No."

Do you believe that you will succeed? Do you think that you can do it? If not, I'm very sorry, but you won't. It's just that simple. It all starts with a belief. Look no further than the insane patient's rants to figure out why you don't seem to be able to work on your business, lose the muffin top or feel happy.

You are free to create exactly what you want, and allow in something even better. How? Follow this simple FREE process:

» F- Find the insane patient's belief that is not serving you. "You'll never pull that off," or "Who do you think you are trying to do that, " or even "There's way too much on your plate to consider that," are examples.

» R- Reduce your suffering by replacing the thought. As you are watching your thoughts, ask Girl Interrupted to have a seat. Pivot your attention toward a positive thought that you believe and that makes you feel better.

» E- Encourage yourself to take one tiny step toward the result that you want.

» E- Enjoy life without the mental drama. Keep the patient well rested, well fed, and have some fun.

By practicing this FREE technique, the obstacles melt, opportunities show up and brilliant you gets to taste your surprise center.

Yummo!

Queen Latifah Sings to Me

Queen Latifah, Nelly and Colbie Callait take turns coaching me when I run. I've been running now for about 5-6 months and am training for a half marathon in October. This is big news and a magnificent obsession in my life. Great discovery: the "runner's high" does exist and is a fun byproduct of taking care of myself. When I am not running with my kick ass friend Jill, I turn on my ipod to make my run even more fun. That's where my celebrity posse enters and I borrow lines from their music to create motivating thoughts for myself.

Notice that I said, "**create** motivating thoughts.'

Motivation will not knock on your door and come snuggle in bed with you. It will not tap you on the shoulder and invite you to get up off of the couch. It will not interrupt your gossip session to remind you that you have an appointment with yourself. It can only be found within you. Motivation is a feeling state that you create yourself.

It's the coolest thing to realize that you can create any feeling state that you want your very own self. Happiness, peace, calm, exhilaration, confidence, passion. And, it doesn't even matter if your brother just punked you on Facebook, or if your cat peed on your fresh dry cleaning. You get to decide what you will feel. How? Two questions:

How do you want to feel?

What would you need to think and then do to feel that way?

Yesterday I wanted to feel motivated to run. My mind created lots of excuses as to why running was not a good idea: you do not have enough time, it is too hot, you can wait until tomorrow, your favorite running skirt is dirty.

I laughed.

And then I decided that I would think this instead: your body wants to move, there is always enough time, it is hot but I can handle it, my second favorite running skirt is clean.

And then, I called on my celebrity running posse and let them sing motivating songs to me.

Read some of the lyrics and see if you agree that I couldn't help but leave it all on the pavement with this running though my head.

Something Special by Colbie Callait

I found a way to be everything
I've dreamed of,
and I know it's in me
that I will become
who I want to be
and I finally found it and I'm taking the long way out
Cause it's going to be, something special to me
Something special to me
Days go by and I grow stronger
It takes time, but I'll never let go
Days go by and I'll try harder to make it mine, I know…
It's something special to me

What are you listening to?

Getting What You Want

Ask the questions that can move you forward

"I never get what I want, and it sucks!" My client was almost as irritated as I had been when Ray the Beagle, then a puppy, chewed through a Lands' End shipping box and used four pairs of new leather school shoes as teething rings. Almost.

Martha Beck, the insanely talented genius who trained me, recently wrote in the first chapter of, The Team, her new book in progress, two questions that she asks herself continuously:

1. How did I get here?

2. What do I do next?

Fabulous questions to ask, especially during one of her retreats in Africa when she was facing a mama rhinoceros that was protecting her young. These questions were practical and useful, given Martha's situation. They were also useful for my client's circumstances.

I find that most people, especially the ones who aren't getting what they want, ask the wrong questions. Instead of the two simple path tweakers above, the decidedly "unlucky" will ask:

1. Who did this to me?

2. Who is going to fix this for me?

Notice the difference? Hint: the second set of questions is victim like. No sense of independence or of living as a creator.

We can relearn how to create what we want from kids. Take my 9-year-old daughter, Emily, for example. Sassiness on wheels, she continuously astounds me with her resourcefulness. Despite being born into our clearly crazy family, and the fact that she has a life coach for a mother, she thrives.

Several months ago, Emily asked me if she could have a "girl dog." Apparently, I hadn't noticed the huge problem that all of our pets (2 beagles, 1 cat, 2 ferrets and 1 hamster) were all male. The horror. I politely declined her invitation (over and over and over again) to add another thing that pees to our family.

She kept asking. She got more creative in her requests and propositions. Until one day, I took her bait. If you've ever read my blog or Facebook status updates, you know that Jake, our skinny Beagle, is a challenging subject. He's not exactly bringing home trophies from obedience training. So when Emily offered to train Jake in exchange for getting a girl puppy, I agreed. Of course! This is a deal that I cannot lose! Train JAKE?! I laughed. She asked why I did not have faith in her. I told her that I had truckloads of faith in her, just not in her subject. I underestimated both of them.

Emily bought a booked called Dog Training for Dummies, watched my DVD's of the Dog Whisperer, and bought special liver treats for her training experiment. We agreed on five tricks that she would teach Jake. Once Jake could consistently sit, stay, beg, drop, and do a circle trick, we would know that Emily had done her job.

I was so amused by her optimism.

A few days later, I was attending a "graduation ceremony" for Jake, complete with a special certificate Emily made him.

The darned dog was actually trainable! And Emily had done it! It was Emily's turn for amusement. Now I am shopping for a girl puppy.

The lessons here are both simple and profound:

1. Ask yourself constantly: How did I get here, and what will I do next? Stop waiting for other people to solve your issues for you. It's your life. Live it. Ask yourself powerful questions to create a vision.

2. Create a plan. Come up with tiny steps to inch toward your vision.

3. Celebrate! When you reach your vision, enjoy it!

4. Never underestimate the magic of strong intentions. Find. A. Way.

Leave Barking to the Puppies

What would happen, if just for today, you decided to stop:

complaining

whining

stalling

tantruming

crazy towning

bluffing

gossiping

judging

excuse-ifying

the crap.

What if instead of barking your way around the edges of your comfort zone, you reached for something better?

What could you create in the time that you just spent moaning and groaning?

Accept what is. Create what's next. I'll be there cheering for you.

I Feel Like I've Been Hit By An SUV

How to Survive Crappy Life Circumstances

A rusty, black SUV ran over my 9-month-old puppy, Juliet. She was hit so hard, I didn't think she'd get up off of the pavement. In that split second of fearless puppy abandon and burning brake smell, things that really matter became even more apparent. Unexpected trauma usually makes what's important crystal clear.

Unfolded laundry, a new patio, the right heels didn't seem to matter much.

What did matter was saving the life of a sweet, gentle Cavalier King Charles Spaniel with a spunky, loving charm. Your life, too, is worth saving.

Happiness doesn't reside in pain-free homes and perfect souls. It simmers and marinates even in the midst of rude school-pick-up-line moms, lost careers, and snarky hateration (rude people so filled with hateful thoughts that they try to bring you down).

If you find yourself wondering how the hell you are going to survive the current painful page in your life, this is how to get through so that you can create your next chapter.

Get Up, Even When It Hurts

Rusty black was caught off guard and hit her. Hard. She rolled. The rear tire hit her, again. Scared and road burned, Juliet still managed to get up and scamper into the bushes.

Healing begins by deciding to just get up. Where are you lying down in your life? You aren't road kill. Lift yourself up. Pick a small and specific-enough step to begin today.

Come Out of Hiding, Even If It's Scary.

She didn't want to come out. She cried and howled and raced through the bushes trying to find her way back home. I had to crawl on my belly through the bushes so that she could hear my voice and see my outstretched arms. She couldn't walk out but, with a little help from me, she did.

I believe that—especially when we are struggling—a thousand angels are conspiring to help us. Take the outstretched hand, answer the email offering to help, return the phone call from a friend, accept support in any way it shows up. Accepting support is much less scary than doing it alone.

Hang Tough, Even When You'd Rather Not

Three pelvic fractures can make anyone cranky. And yet, she manages to wag her tail at us. Reminds me of the famous Winston Churchill quote, "If you're going through hell, keep going."

How can you make it better for yourself? Find a reason to wag your tail with this Rx:

1. Gratitude List – Make a list of five things you are grateful for in your life. Watch your mood shift.

2. Rest. It takes some time heal. There's a whole lot of productivity that happens when you rest. Necessary. Do it.

3. Come up with three tweaks for your life. Create three crazy-simple and specific changes that you can start on right now. Not something so overwhelming that you'll "wait until Monday" to try. Think, "Walk around the block for ten minutes on M, W, and F at 8:30 a.m.," instead of "exercise more." (This is lovingly stolen from my coaching colleague and cool friend, Bridgette Boudreau.)

Yes, we have a lot to learn from our animal loves, and puppy Juliette teaches me what puts the Cavalier in the Cavalier King Charles breed. She inspires me lift my head up and find a way. 'Cause really, is there any other option that makes sense?

Are you smarter than a 4th Grader?

I'm going to call bullshit when I hear it.

'Cause guess what? I don't believe you. And you don't believe you either. That's why you've got one hand in the donut-hole bag, and the other holding your credit card for retail therapy.

Because we always know

It's not too hard. You are enough. You have learned enough to do your thing. We might not want to face why we aren't exercising or having fun or building our business, but deep down we KNOW when we aren't doing things that serve us. There's nothing else "out there" that will solve what's going on "in here."

Are you smarter than a 4th Grader?

My 9-year-old daughter, Emily, continues to inspire me about how to live fully. She auditioned and earned a role in "The Lion King" at school.

These little thespians practice on Monday mornings at 6:30 a.m. Yep, you read that correctly: 6:30 a.m. on MONDAYS.

On Sunday, Emily reminded me three times that she needed to leave for school an hour early to attend practice. Monday morning, I was all interested in getting my green smoothie on, and spaced out about the time. At 6:15a.m., I looked at the clock, and realized we should already be leaving the house. I had not even gotten her out of bed yet!

I bolted up the stairs, woke her up, and asked her to please hurry. Now, let me interject here that most school mornings I have to practically threaten my kids with jail time in a Turkish prison (or folding laundry) to get them out of bed. Ninety seconds later, she was dressed, teeth and hair brushed, shoes on, snack bar in hand, ready to roll out the door. I was scrambling for my shoes and keys. Whaaaaaat?

What's the difference? She is motivated, engaged, having fun, and loving play practice. It's quickly rivaling painting as her thing. She wants to be there. I woke her up 45 minutes late? No problem. Her hair was wonky? No problem. She didn't get her chocolate chip pancakes?

Who cares!

I seriously laughed the whole way to the school, thinking about the example she demonstrated for me. This is exactly what it looks like when your beliefs, passion, intention and action line up. When you have that fire in your belly to do something, you are unstoppable. Excuses fall away.

If your pilot light is out, you can get your fire back. It's never too late.

1. **STOP** hopping from diet to diet, program to program, guru to guru. You are your own guru. All that seeking is exhausting. Your answers are right there. What do you think, if you had to guess, that you are DYING to tell yourself?

2. **LOOK** around at the ideas, tools and strategies that you already have at your disposal. Pick one thing that you can tweak today, and one idea of where you want to go next. Get going. One step at a time.

3. **LISTEN** to your body compass and your higher self for guidance.

You don't need a color-by-numbers plan. "Do this exactly as I say and you'll get that." "Eat according to this plan, and beat yourself thin, and you'll get a hot body in 7 days." (and a hot mess of a mind.)

Someone else's plan will get you someone else's life, business, body, and thoughts. I don't think you want to trade your uncertainty for failed impersonation. You answers aren't there. They are inside of you.

Don't be afraid of your fire; it won't burn you. Excuses will.

What do you regret?

Scott's Aunt Jane died a few days ago. She was 94 when she passed, and lived a long beautiful life as an independent woman. At her funeral showing yesterday, I couldn't help but wonder as she neared the end of her human existence, if she mentally filed through regrets, or if she drifted away with deep satisfaction. Pictures lined up of Emily Jane as a baby, a school girl, a young woman. What were her dreams? Did she go after them? I never asked her.

We've had quite a few family happenings this year that have led me swimming deeper into life's questions about purpose, meaning and passion. My brother-in-law Shawn had a stroke. He's recovering well, and it's a true testament to what the human spirit can accomplish, if willing and motivated, to watch him be strong and balanced enough to help carry Jane's casket at the funeral.

So, all this mortality in my face has me considering things. What are the top five regrets people have on their deathbeds?

According to a fantastic article I read in TNW Lifehacks, they are:

1. I wish I had the courage to live my life how I wanted, instead of how others expected me to live.

2. I wish that I had worked less, or not so hard.

3. I wish that I had the courage to express my feelings.

4. I wish that I had stayed in touch with my friends.

5. I wish that I had allowed myself to be happier.

These are issues that I coach clients on daily. I listen to the fears and excuses, and help shape shift them into connection, relationships, work that matters, and peace without using food, alcohol, shopping, gossip, or business to self medicate.

Life is too short to substitute what you want with brownies, work, boots or a packed schedule.

So, I ask you, given your health, genetics, family history, if you had to guess, *how old do you think you will be when you pass away?*

How old are you now?

How many years does that leave for you here on earth?

Let that number sink in. And, now, let's get to work on how you want to spend those years.

If no one would care or object, if money were of no issue, if you had enough time, if you believed you could do it, what would you do with the rest of your life? Would you learn to swim? Travel? Tell THE ONE that you love her desperately? Work less? Brainstorm for ten minutes.

Now, let's set about to do it.

Do not make whiney bullshit excuses. Your soul has no time for baby talk. If you want, go ahead and list all the reasons your mind has alphabetized as to why you cannot. Go ahead. I'll wait.

Here's what I have to say about your list.

So?

Pick one thing. ONE thing.

Create 3-5 small turtle steps to get it done.

Coach yourself or get coached around your crappy mind crack thinking about it.

I wouldn't challenge you if I didn't know that you could do it. Yes, you can. You are on the edge of glory.

Am I Living a Life Worth Writing About?

This seems to be the question that I ponder as I write about, and talk about, and teach on life lessons. You see, I'm not just interested in philosophizing about life. I am deeply committed to taking what I learn, doing something with it, and then helping others do the same.

Of course, the answer is yes. Our lives are all valuable beyond measure. Just because. But, **what kind of story will our lives tell**? That is the deeper question. We become so distracted by schedules, lists, smart phones and a grim reaper level of obligations, that we miss simple miracles happening every day. We worry about life, but we do not truly live it in the face of so much busy.

Did I tell you that I'm going sky diving?

I do not want to only watch YouTube videos on how to sky dive, I want to experience it. Reading a book on how to make a green smoothie is not the same as making and tasting one. **Sitting around and talking about what you do not like and railing against the machine will only get you bummer-cited** (Excited in a downer way...Look, I made up another new word!). That's not the same thing at all as being an example of what you do like, and showing others how they can move towards something better. In short, life rewards feel good action, and your outer reflects your inner.

I've been using a terrific tool from Chip and Dan Heath's book, Switch: How to Change When Change is Hard, called **Destination Postcard**. It's my favorite kind of tool: easy to understand, simple to implement, insanely effective. If you'd like to begin creating a life that tells the story that you want to tell, that leads by example, give it a whirl.

1. **Where do you want to experience change in your life?** Pick an area of least satisfaction. Think physical health, spiritual life, relationships, career, time. But just pick one for now. I know you want to drop 20,

make more money, have hot sex and reach nirvana right now, but we are pacing ourselves here.

2. **Select a time frame for change**. It could be 30 days, 60 days, 6 months, one year, 5 years from now.

3. Imagine that your FUTURE SELF has already lined up with this goal. It's a done deal, girl. In the bag. As your future self, **write and send your current self a little post card from the victory party**. It should be short enough to fit on a post card. Ok, maybe you'll send a jumbo post card, but keep it short and sweet.

I'll show you mine if you show me yours.

Dear Susan,

You will not believe what it's like to spend the summer of 2012 in Europe. The deep connection we've had with the family, the pure bliss of seeing the world in person, and the inspiration on rocket fuel is something that I can hardly use words to explain. Congratulations for spending time planning the logistics, saving the money, and devising a way to work from anywhere. The Hyatt Riot has learned so much, felt so intensely, and grown beyond measure.

Can't wait for you to get here!

Love,

Me

If you want to share your post cards on the blog, I'd love it. And, if you want to mail me one, I'll help create some amped up space for your dream to live. (Susan Hyatt 714 S Willow Road, Evansville, IN 47714)

Afterword

Lucky People Hang Together!

I started writing this book when my kids were just 9 and 11. So much has happened in two years. So much luck created.

One of my greatest strengths is that I'm a boot wearing idea factory. Some days, I wish I could temper it. Other days, I just let it flow. This book and the worksheets in it are a result of the flow.

Keep up to date on my latest ideas for you at www.shyatt.com. You can join my lucky tribe by registering there. You'll get free stuff, and be the first to know about what's happening.

I hold daily luck parties on Facebook at http://www.facebook.com/susan. ohyatt. The Hyatt Riot has to routinely say, "DON'T PUT THAT ON FACEBOOK!" because I over share.

Get the worksheets from the book, a free MP3 of the Get Your Lucky On song that I had exclusively written and recorded by the fabulous McCall Erikson for you. It's a luck booster for sure, here http://www. createyourownluckbook.com.

Acknowledgements

I spent 2008 trying to figure out which topic to write about. Eventually, I ran away and had a two-year romance with my definition of luck. And there's a whole community who helped me to create it.

My husband of 18 years, Scott Hyatt, has always been my lucky coach. He's this really badass combo of "make it happen, but make sure you have fun at the same time." Every gutsy move I ever made before the age of 25 was because he told me I could do it.

Margie Oglesbee, my southern mama, used to always tell me that I could "get glad just as easy as I got mad." Enlightenment from Savannah. She's the best kind of mom.

Ellen LuCree Dobson, my maternal grandmother, who was the one to tell me "where there's a will, there's a way." It's the foundation of everything that I do.

My grade school English teachers, Mrs. Scafidi and Mrs. Daniels, who encouraged me to write. For my high school graduation, Mrs. Scafidi gave me a writing journal with the inscription: "Compose your first book here!" Finding that journal the same day I was considering starting my book was a wink from God that I'll never forget. And, way back in 1987, Mrs. Daniels said, "If you do not grow up to do something where you write and are creative for a living, I just don't know anything at all." Look Mrs. Daniels, I did it!

The backbone of my business, the people who create the space for me to do what I do, and then pick up the pieces behind me, is comprised of the amazing and incomparable Jessica Reisenbeck and Sandra Trca-Black. Thank you for making my life easier.

My publisher, Angela Lauria, who once sent me an email and said that "I deserved to hold the finished book in my hands." You have no idea how that motivated me to keep on writing.

Glad Doggett, who jumped in at the final hour, literally, and helped edit my manuscript. Without her, you would be reading even more southern ghetto language than what appears on these pages. Kelly Johnson also joined in with just a few hours to spare to help me refine things. A million thank yous to you both.

Martha Beck. There are almost no words. Some random hellish day in real estate in February 2007, I picked up Finding Your Own North Star. The luckiest day of my life. Thank you for teaching me, mentoring me, and reading my rough drafts. You've made me a better person, and a better writer. I am forever grateful.

Bridgette Boudreau has been my coach, my friend and my sounding board. Inappropriate emails, text messages, and phone calls exchanged kept me laughing and sane. The words thank you seem inadequate.

My good pal Jackie Gartman for being the model of what it is like to parent with intention and laugh like a hyena. You are a great source of fun and inspiration for me.

Many thanks that date all the way back to 2007, to Brooke Castillo. Props for relentlessly asking, "Where's your book?" And, thank you for reading my early work and mentoring me along the way.

My Evansville lucky tribe, Jill Hall, Frances Cadora, Karen Meacham and Stacey Shanks. You girls provide endless laughs, support, and love that is rare.

Special thank you to my sister Teri, who doesn't always get what the heck I am doing or talking about, but who supports me anyway. I lucked up getting a sister like her.

And finally, to my Hyatt Riot. Ryan and Emily Hyatt are walking, talking pieces of my heart. Ryan, who teaches me fierceness and courage, and Emily who teaches me innovation and intuition, are my true lucky charms. Thank you for "being quiet" and "not interrupting" my coaching calls, tele-courses and writing time. And, thank you when you did interrupt. Some of my best memories while writing this book are of the real life lucky examples that you gave me, which is better than fiction material. You two are, without a doubt, the reason I was put on this earth. I am lucky to be your mother. (And, yes, I know you are rolling your eyes right now. It's ok. When you are older you might be touched by this.)

About the Author

Susan Hyatt, owner of Ideal Life Design, is an author, public speaker, retreat facilitator, and Master Certified Martha Beck Life Coach. Trained and certified by Dr. Martha Beck—a monthly columnist to O, The Oprah Magazine and guest on The Oprah Show—Susan uses innovative techniques to help clients identify goals, remove obstacles, and design their ideal lives.

Known for her energy, honesty, and ability to get things done for herself and her clients, Susan was hand selected by Dr. Martha Beck to run her Life Coach Training program, and Master Life Coaching program in 2008-2010. Susan currently leads classes and teaches the Beck curriculum to life coaches in training.

Susan's widely recognized for her non-diet approach to permanent weight loss, and her work helping women lose the diet mentality while achieving their natural weight. She's also passionate about helping entrepreneurs create businesses that change the world.

O, The Oprah Magazine featured Susan in the LifeCoach Coffee Chat campaign with Seattle's Best Coffee.

Susan is crazy-in-the-eyes serious about helping clients create a life they love through individual and group coaching, retreats and writing.

Susan is the mother of two hilarious kids, Ryan age 12, and Emily age 10, and a wife of 18 years to a very patient husband, Scott. She lovingly refers to her family as "The Hyatt Riot." When she isn't having a ridiculous amount of fun working with clients, you can find her running, cycling, hanging out with her family, writing, or reading. To learn more about her coaching programs, visit www.shyatt.com.

Want to Really Get Lucky?

It's my highest intention that you are able to use the exercises outlined in this book and make clear, fun and intentional change in your life. If you'd like to dive deep into this material, I have a number of live and home study luck opportunities for you. Just visit www.shyatt.com to get your lucky on!

Private Coaching

One on one coaching transformed my life. It can do the same for you. Having someone in your corner, whose sole purpose is to help you make good things happen, is a nearly religious experience. I am not kidding you. Get coached and watch miracles happen. www.shyatt.com/coaching

Group Telecourses

There's something really special about getting coached in a group environment from the comfort of your own space. The energy, the community, the camaraderie, the results. Check out the Lucky Circles that pop up quarterly and join us by phone from anywhere in the world.

Live Workshops and Retreats

It's a real treat for me to meet and work with my readers and clients in person. A few times a year, I lead exclusive retreats and live events. Be on the first to know list, by registering on my site to receive my newsletter. I announce opportunities likes these to my tribe list first. You can do that at www.shyatt.com.

Lucky Living Products

Want to learn this material at your own pace with guided help? Check out my products page for at home support that will make your laptop, ipod and ipad smile. www.shyatt.com/products.

Create Your Own Luck Resource Page

Martha Beck, Best Selling Author of Finding Your Own North Star and Steering By Starlight, www.marthabeck.com.

L.P. Hartley, The Go Between, The New York Review of Books.

Jill Bolte Taylor, PhD., My Stroke of Insight: A Brain Scientist's Personal Journey, www.drjilltaylor.com.

Kathy Vick, Run Like a Girl: Igniting the Spark for your Next Great Adventure, www.runlikeagirl.org.

Garth Stein, The Art of Racing in The Rain, www.garthstein.com.

Jessica Steward, Master Certified Martha Beck™ Life Coach, www.stewardcoaching.com.

Kimberly Kingsley, The Energy Cure, www.kimberlykingsley.com

Pam Slim, Escape from Cubicle Nation: From Corporate Prisoner to Thriving Entrepreneur, www.escapefromcubiclenation.com.

Gary Zukav, The Seat of the Soul , www.garyzukav.wwwhubs.com.

Kirsten Marion, http://www.theenergeticsofwealth.com/

Seattle's Best Coffee #3, www.seattlesbest.com.

Texts from God, www.textsfromgod.com.

Susan Hyatt, Jacked Up on Greens, www.shyatt.com/smoothiebook.

Jeremie Kubicek, Leadership is Dead: How Influence is Reviving It, www.jeremiekubicek.com.

Maya Angelou, www.mayaangelou.com.

Koelle Simpson, Master Certified Martha Beck™ Life Coach and Horse Whisperer, www.koelleinc.com.

Honey Badger, www.youtube.com, type 'honey badger randall' in the search box. BEWARE of offensive language!

Fabeku Fatunmise, Business Awesomizer, Suck Exorcist, Punk Rock Alchemist, www.sankofasong.com.

Lisa Sonora Beam, The Creative Entrepreneur, www.lisasonorabeam.com

Paulo Coelho, The Alchemist, www.paulocoelho.com.

Ingrid Arna, www.mybodylovediet.com

Sir Winston Churchill, from a speech given at Harvard University on September 6. 1943.

Robert Fritz, The Path of Least Resistance , www.robertfritz.com.

Special Thanks to these Create Your Own Luck

Contributors & Supporters

Tom Hawley	Jen Beckman
Gail Larsen	Linda Ford
Yvonne Cranmer	Maria Dolson-Verroye
Sarah Moore	Laura Wagner
Melissa Heisler	Gretchen Pisano
Lisa Bendzak	Sarah Bamford Seidelmann
Tracy Braunstein	Elise Touchette
Scott Dallner	David Wu
Teri Proffitt	Maggie Laura McReynolds
Danielle Erley	Lisa Benesh
Kelli Seaton	Diane Hunter
Pamela Dravicszki	Maria Frias
Joy Tanksley	Gail Kenney
Anthony Bouoard	Frances Cadora
Andrea Owen	Sarah Yost
Tracee Sioux	Meghan Currie
Kelly Pratt	Kanesha Baynard
Fabeku Fatunmise	Laurie Hawley
Gaynor Levisky	Beth Herman
Kelly Johnson	Danette Butler
Lori Barlow	Patricia Neal
Pedro Baez	Debby Werthman
Sabrina Holden	Rose Regier
Heidi Loren	Jennifer Young
Valerie Steiger	Tanya Geisler
Rhonda Gassman	Deb Smouse

How to get your Free Gifts!

As a way of saying thanks for buying Create Your Own Luck, we are pleased to offer you $292.07 worth of FREE Gifts to accompany the book. Throughout the book, author Susan Hyatt offers Lucky Lab worksheets to help you create your own luck. Susan has also made available companion videos for each chapter and songwriter McCall Erickson wrote a special song just for you!

When you register at www.CreateYourOwnLuckBook.com, you'll receive all the following Lucky Items:

»	Lucky Song	Get Your Lucky On by Songwriter McCall Erickson
»	Lucky Lab#1	Scientist in Your Life
»	Lucky Lab #2	Track the Triggers
»	Lucky Lab #3	Got Babemba?
»	Lucky Lab #4	The Talent Ferret
»	Lucky Lab #5	Envy Buster
»	Lucky Lab #6	The Happy Basket
»	Lucky Lab #7	Passion Formula
»	Lucky Lab #8	Be Your Own Fun Coordinator
»	Lucky Lab #9	Dial it Up
»	Lucky Lab #10	Texts from God
»	Lucky Lab #11	The Anti-Leotard Exercise Program
»	Lucky Lab #12	What's Your End Game?
»	Lucky Lab #13	Play to Your Edge
»	Lucky Lab #14	Line Up Key Areas
»	Lucky Lab #15	Line Up with Your Brilliance
»	Lucky Lab #16	Inspiration Junction for Creativity
»	Lucky Lab #17	What's Your Flavor of Fun?
»	Lucky Video 1	How to Rock Your Day Using the Dial It Up Method!
»	Lucky Video 2	Interview on Passion with Jessica Steward
»	Lucky Video 3	Interview on Energy with Kimberly Kingsley
»	Lucky Video 4	Luck, Leadership and Wealth, Interview with Kirsten Marion
»	Lucky Video 5	Creativity and Luck Interview with Lisa Sonora Beam
»	Lucky Video 6	Have more Fun and get Luckier, Interview with Ingrid Arna
»	Lucky Bonus	The Lucky 7 Manifesto

**Go to www.CreateYourOwnLuckBook.com
to download your free gifts today!**

The Lucky 7

1. LIFE DOES NOT HAVE TO BE HARD. Or grueling, or constricting, or sluggish, or cruel. Right now. Or ever. You can think yourself free. 2. WORK DOES NOT HAVE TO FEEL LIKE A PRISON. It can feel like connection, exploration, divination... play. Like when you were a kid. And you can still pay your mortgage. 3. LUCK DOES NOT HAVE TO BE A MYSTERY. It can be something you create, with intention — not a passive occurrence. You can actually invite it into your life — for good. 4. YOUR FREAK FLAG IS EVERYONE'S FAVORITE PART (OF YOU). Seriously. We're waiting (with bated breath) for you to whip it out + wave it proud. Just you wait for the thunderous applause. 5. YOU CAN HAVE WHATEVER YOU WANT. Or some delicious flavor of it. And you don't have to wait until you're retired to rent an RV and travel the world. In fact, please don't. I'm begging you. 6. YOUR DREAM IS AS VALUABLE AS ANYONE ELSES. Whether you're designing the world's biggest cupcake or the world's most efficient vacuum cleaner, it's your CALLING, babe! Let it howl! 7. ASKING FOR WHAT YOU WANT IS WILD! Whether it's a massive raise, or just a sprinkle of cocoa on your cappuccino, clear requests garner rapid results. And the ripple effects are beyond imagining.

10444259R00089

Made in the USA
Charleston, SC
05 December 2011